SPECIFIC INTENT

O'NEIL DE NOUX

SPECIFIC INTENT

O'NEIL DE NOUX

PINNACLE BOOKS
WINDSOR PUBLISHING CORP.

PINNACLE BOOKS are published by

Windsor Publishing Corp.
475 Park Avenue South
New York, NY 10016

ISBN 1-55817-754-X

Printed in the United States of America

For Frenchy

"First Degree Murder is the killing of a human being when the offender has specific intent to kill or to inflict great bodily harm and is engaged in the perpetration or attempted perpetration of aggravated kidnapping, aggravated escape, aggravated arson, aggravated rape, aggravated burglary, armed robbery, or simple robbery; When the offender has specific intent to kill or to inflict great bodily harm upon a fireman or peace officer engaged in the performance of his lawful duties; When the offender has specific intent to kill or to inflict great bodily harm upon more than one person or; when the offender has specific intent to kill or inflict great bodily harm and has offered, has been offered, has given, or has received anything of value for the killing; When the offender has specific intent to kill or to inflict great bodily harm upon a victim under the age of twelve years." — Louisiana Criminal Code, 1985

This is a true story. Some names have been changed to protect the innocent and to avoid frivolous lawsuits.

Crime scene photos taken by Crime Scene Technician William Viera.

Aerial photos taken by Crime Scene Technician Charles Young.

SPECIFIC INTENT

O'NEIL DE NOUX

Part One

"She had her hair in braids, on either side. She looked precious."

One

The white Chevrolet cruised back and forth, with no apparent motive, through the streets of Terrytown. Like a shark, the Chevrolet meandered, turning at will until it came to a stop against the curb next to a children's playground near the Tres Vidas Apartment Complex. The four occupants of the car did not move aimlessly; their intent was purposeful.

The driver, twenty-one-year-old John Francis Wille, turned off the ignition and leaned back in his seat. Billy Phillips climbed out of the backseat of the car and stretched. Billy, at twenty-five, looked young for his age, with boyish good looks, sandy hair, and blue eyes. He was joined outside the car by fourteen-year-old Sheila Renee Walters, who had also been in the backseat of the car. Sheila brushed back her straight blond hair with her hands as she climbed out. Sheila's mother, Judith Walters, remained in the

11

front seat with John, taking the opportunity to lie down.

It was a hot Sunday, one of those sweltering Louisiana summer days when the temperature neared three digits, matched by near triple digit humidity. There wasn't even a hint of breeze in Terrytown, a residential suburb directly across the Mississippi from downtown New Orleans.

Billy smiled at Sheila and told her to follow him into the apartment complex, so he could point out a little girl to her. John climbed out and fanned his sticky shirt as he leaned restlessly against the front fender of the Chevrolet. This allowed Judith to stretch out across the front seat. She kicked several empty Bourbon bottles out of the way. John was a burly man, about 5'10" tall, with dark brown eyes and long, curly, brown hair that had not been washed in days. John sported several days' growth of beard on his square face and a twelve-inch butcher knife in his boot. His deep set eyes gave him the appearance of a Neanderthal.

Judith felt John's weight as he leaned against the car. Opening her eyes momentarily, she noticed trees and power lines overhead. She was thinking that the sun was so bright and hot.

Billy stopped halfway through the complex and grabbed Sheila's arm. "That's her," he said, pointing to a little girl by the pool. "I want her," he said.

He went back to the car, while Sheila went for the little girl.

Jodee Lopatta woke shortly before 10:00 A.M. She found two of her daughters downstairs in the apartment. Eight-year-old Nichole and her little sister, Samantha, were watching television.

"Where's your sister?" she asked the girls.

"Jodee Bee's still asleep," Nichole answered.

Jodee's oldest daughter, also named Jodee, was eleven. Everyone called her Jodee Bee. A few minutes later, when Jodee Bee came downstairs, she discovered they were out of cereal. She asked her mother if she could go to a nearby convenience store called Cowboy's to get some Froot Loops. Jodee gave her daughter a five dollar bill. All three daughters left together.

When they returned, Jodee Bee had also bought chocolate-covered doughnuts. The Lopatta family then had breakfast together. During breakfast, Nichole's grandmother Eleanor Mallory came downstairs. Nichole asked if she should wake Mark up for some cereal. Her mother said no.

Gunnery Sergeant Mark Summers had spent the night on the Lopatta couch, sleeping off a good night's drinking. It was unusual for Mark, or anyone, to spend the night on the couch, but it had been Saturday night and Mark had come over to spill his worries out to his friend. Jodee, a Yeoman Third class in the Navy, wasn't about to let her friend drive home after drinking. Mark and his wife, like Jodee

13

Lopatta and her husband, were separated; only Mark had a new girlfriend, and the troubles that went along with a divorce and a new love were sometimes too much. He had needed a sympathetic ear.

When Mark did wake up around 11:00 A.M., he drove Jodee to pick up her car, which had been repaired on Saturday. Jodee Bee and Samantha went along for the ride. Nichole stayed behind to watch television with her grandmother. Jodee stopped by the grocery store on her way home and bought, among other items, some fresh bing cherries. Nichole loved fresh cherries.

Fixing lunch later at around 2:00 P.M., Jodee had to tell Nichole that she couldn't just eat cherries. After lunch, the Lopatta girls went out to play with their friends from the apartments, two sisters named Pepper and Dawn. Jodee put on a Barbra Streisand tape, sat on the couch, and opened a book. Shortly before 4:00 P.M., Jodee's good friend Carline Thayer came by. The girls came in, too, for more cherries.

The women began talking about their respective spouses. Jodee asked the girls to go outside, but they wanted to listen. So Jodee had an idea. She told her friend, "Come on, I need some bread. Why don't we go to Delchamps?"

Jodee grabbed her purse and told her mother she was leaving for a while. Eleanor nodded. On their way out, Jodee told Carline, "Let's go get some iced tea or something." So they could talk. But before

14

they could escape, Samantha began crying because her mama was leaving. Jodee picked up her youngest daughter, comforted Samantha, and then sent her off with her sister to play upstairs.

"I'm hungry," Carline said as the two women left.

"Want to stop at Po Folks?" Jodee suggested.

The women drove directly to the restaurant, located at the corner of Behrman and Belle Chasse Highway. They ordered iced teas first and then chicken and steak, mashed potatoes, and green beans. Po Folks was a family restaurant chain that specialized in home cooked Southern cuisine. Over their meals, the women talked about their husbands, about their troubles, about men in general.

After her mother had left, Nichole went out to sit next to the swimming pool and eat some more fresh cherries. She noticed a pretty teenage girl with blond hair approaching. Nichole looked up and smiled at the girl. The girl stopped and said, "Hi, my name is Sheila."

"Hi," Nichole answered.

"Do you know Billy Phillips?"

"No."

"Well, do you want to meet him?"

Nichole shrugged. The girl with the blond hair was so pretty.

"Billy says he knows you."

"He does?"

Sheila nodded.

Nichole got up and walked off with Sheila. On the way to the white Chevrolet, Nichole grabbed Sheila's hand.

Judith heard John's voice. He said, "My, aren't you a pretty one. Who do you take after, your mommy or your daddy?"

Peeking up, Judith saw her daughter standing with a little girl with honey-colored hair. They were holding hands. The little girl was looking at John and smiling.

"This is my mother," Sheila said, pointing to Judith. "And this is John. And this is Billy Phillips."

John spoke next. He asked the little girl, "Do you want to go to the store with us?"

"For how long?"

"Only a couple minutes," he answered. Then he told everyone to get in. Billy climbed into the backseat. Sheila followed, moving Nichole in ahead of her. Judith lay back down and closed her eyes. John started up the Chevrolet and pulled away from the curb.

A few minutes later, Judith noticed someone kicking the back of the seat and looked over the seat to see the little girl with the honey hair sitting between Billy and Sheila. Judith looked away from the little girl's wide eyes because she knew why the little girl was there. Earlier, when John had picked up Billy hitchhiking, the two men had a long talk about having sex with a little girl. Billy said he knew a girl who

16

lived on the West Bank, a girl he'd had sex with before, but he wasn't sure where she lived exactly. When they couldn't find that particular girl, they settled on whoever they could find.

When the girl said something about going home, Judith looked at her boyfriend's face. John Francis Wille's square jaw was set. He stared straight ahead. She knew he was upset. She knew it had started, the frenzy had begun. She could see his hands gripping the steering wheel like a vise. Judith closed her eyes again.

A few minutes later, she heard the little girl crying, "Where's my mommy?"

John's voice boomed like a shotgun blast. "SHUT UP!"

Judith sat up. Sheila jumped at the noise and nervously began playing a hand game with the little girl.

The little girl continued crying. Between sobs, she managed to say, "I want to go home."

"NO!" John shouted.

Reaching back quickly, John slapped the little girl hard across her face. A streak of bright blood oozed from the girl's mouth.

Two

Sunday, June 2, 1985, 8:19 P.M.

Operator seventy-six of the Jefferson Parish Sheriff's Office answered the phone after the second ring, "Sheriff's Office. Seventy-six."

"Ah, yes. Do you have a deputy by the name of Louis Dufour?" Jodee Lopatta asked.

"Yes, hon. We do."

"Okay, is there any way that you possibly can get, uh, a message to him over the radio?"

"If he's on duty, ma'am."

"Yes, he's on duty. Ah . . ." Jodee had just seen Louis, in his marked police car, by the apartments, when she'd returned from Po Folks.

"Where does he work?" the operator asked.

"Pardon me?"

"What district does he work in?"

"I . . . I don't know what district exactly he

18

works in, but he works in the bomb squad." Louis never told Jodee what district.

"Hold on. Let me see if he's on the line up."

The operator put Jodee on hold. Jodee was thinking, *They should be able to find Louis. He is working.* The operator seemed to take a long time.

After looking through all of the Jefferson Parish Sheriff's Duty Rosters, the operator came back on the line, "Hello ma'am."

"Yes?"

"I don't see him on the lineup."

"Okay. Well, I know he works for Jefferson Parish. Is this the central office for all Jefferson Parish?"

"This is the radio room, ma'am."

"All right. The reason is, I know the man, and my daughter's been missing for the last three hours."

"Uh, huh. Well, ma'am. Would you like to make a police report?"

Jodee let out a nervous sigh. "Well, I guess I'd better." Her voice began to shake.

"What is the location?" the operator asked.

"All right," Jodee fought to control her voice, "it's Tres Vidas, Apartment 95."

"The address?"

"Seven-three-three Carrollwood Village."

Jodee could hear typing in the background, like on a typewriter keyboard.

"Apartment what?"

"Ninety-five."

Jodee could hear more typing. The operator was typing what she was saying.

"What is your name?"

"Lopatta." Jodee spelled it for the operator.

The operator typed each of her answers.

"How old is the child?"

"She's eight. Blond hair. Blue eyes."

"Wait a minute, ma'am." More typing. "Blond hair. Blue eyes. Eight years old. White female?"

"Yes."

"How long has she been missing?"

"Three and a half hours."

"What was she wearing the last time you saw her?"

"Ah! Oh my gosh!" Jodee gasped. Holding the phone receiver away from her mouth, she asked Jodee Bee, "What was she wearing? Do you remember?"

Jodee Bee started to answer her mother, when Jodee remembered what Nichole had on.

"Ah! My gosh! Oh, she's wearing a light blue, okay, she's wearing a light blue T-shirt. She's got a bathing suit and a pair of shorts underneath it. One of those long T-shirts. And she's wearing a light blue, I'm sorry, dark blue sandals. And she's got, ah, the color of hair is like honey blond color." Pause for typing. "She's got blue eyes."

"Is there a building number, ma'am?" *The operator sure had a one-track mind.*

"That's building eight."

"Okay."

"If they come in from Carol Sue, off Behrman Highway, it's the first turn in to Tres Vidas. They take a left and come all the way around the back. And it's the second apartment from the end of the building."

"Okay, ma'am. I'll send someone out."

"All right." Jodee continued to fight to control her voice, "Could you possibly see if you can get a hold of . . . of Louis?"

"Ma'am, we have to send a road deputy that works the area out to the location to make a report."

"Yes, ma'am. I know. But could you possibly do that?"

The operator's voice rose suddenly, "Ma'am, I'm telling you that we cannot do this. He works in a different area."

"All right. Thank you."

Jodee hung up and fought to control herself. This was no time for anger. She had to find Nichole.

Three

Sunday, June 2, 1985, 8:24 P.M.

Deputy Chi Chi Windwehen of the Jefferson Parish Sheriff's Office had just come on duty on the evening watch. Stuffy in her navy blue police uniform, she couldn't wait for the sun to go down. That was the only benefit of the evening watch. The atmospheric temperature would drop, although the temperature of the population never did. Evenings were always popping.

Chi Chi was an attractive woman with long brown hair and dark brown eyes. She was a good officer, who worked easily by herself in her own unit.

When she received a call from headquarters to handle a missing person at the Tres Vidas Apartments, she acknowledged, turned her marked police car around, and drove directly to the apartments. Along the way, she was reminded of her own en-

22

counter with her "missing" son.

Years earlier, when Chi Chi was living in an apartment across the river in Metairie, her four-year-old son had played a prank on her. Seeing his mommy going in and out of the apartment, the boy hid under his bed. He held his laughter as his mother searched for him. Then the boy fell asleep under the bed. Chi Chi frantically searched the entire complex, mobilizing a large search party. Later, when the boy woke, he climbed out, sleepy-eyed, and looked for his mother for a hug. She'd been angry, but relieved to find him.

Arriving at Tres Vidas, Chi Chi parked her unit and went to look for Apartment 95. She had no problem finding it. There was a host of people standing outside the apartment, including a group of children. Maybe, just maybe, the kid was already back, and she wouldn't even have to write a report. But the second she saw the mother, she knew better.

Sitting in the living room, Chi Chi took the information needed for her report, information headquarters needed to issue a bulletin. The deputy expected the family to resist this process. Most families wanted officers to search, and rarely understood the importance of gathering such crucial information needed for the dispatch bulletin.

Chi Chi was surprised by the mother. Although Jodee Lopatta seemed upset that her daughter was missing, she didn't seem at all concerned that the girl had the run of the complex all day. Chi Chi noted that Jodee was a plain-looking woman, about 5'5" tall, with long, light brown hair. She had large hazel eyes that looked more tired than upset.

According to Nichole's sisters, the three girls were outside, playing by the pool, when Nichole "just disappeared." Chi Chi soon discovered, in her questioning, that not only was the mother not watching her children, she wasn't even at the complex when the girl disappeared.

As soon as she finished taking the initial information, Chi Chi gave headquarters the data and began a door-to-door search of the Tres Vidas. Although Jodee Lopatta had already checked with friends around the complex, Chi Chi began the long process of double-checking. She immediately called for assistance.

The swimming pools were checked first as well as the nearby woods and canal. Chi Chi remained on this call for the rest of her shift. She found one potential witness in her canvass, Donald Giordano, a seven-year-old boy who lived in apartment 120. Donald said he saw Nichole in the complex at about 7:30 P.M. She was alone.

Toward the end of the evening watch shift, the patrol supervisor notified the Juvenile Division stand-by officer, in order to turn the case over to the juvenile detectives. Corporal Fred Muller was called out at 11:00 P.M. Upon arriving at Tres Vidas at 11:30 P.M., Muller, a veteran officer known for his thorough, meticulous work, supervised a check of all nearby roads, all empty apartments, the woods, and canal again. Muller sent deputies to knock on every door of buildings 6, 7, 8, 10, 11, and 15. He also called out bloodhounds and the Sheriff's Office Auxiliary Division for assistance.

Setting up a command post in the Lopatta apartment, Muller and other detectives took notice when Jodee Lopatta expressed displeasure at having so many policemen in her apartment. Muller contacted the apartment manager and not only secured the use of a vacant apartment as a command post, but secured a computer printout of all residents of Tres Vidas.

Juvenile Detectives John Mitchell and Howard Wright arrived at the Lopatta apartment to interview the mother and Jodee Bee. Chi Chi watched the juvenile dicks at work. Howard Wright, balding and easygoing, was quiet and businesslike. John Mitchell, a short, black man, rarely at a loss for a strong opinion, appeared sharp in his questions to the mother. Somehow, Chi Chi suspected Mitchell felt as she did, that the mother was inattentive.

At shift change, when Chi Chi and her comrades were being replaced by the midnight shift, she

25

watched the detectives as they continued canvassing the apartments, and still felt angry at the missing girl's mother. Chi Chi felt that, indeed, they would find little Nichole playing in some apartment, long before sunrise. She was, however, bothered by one piece of news she'd received in her canvass of the apartments. Everyone who knew Nichole said she was very friendly and would talk to anyone.

Following investigative procedure, the detectives searched for any known sex offenders or child molesters in the area. They also kept a close eye on the family.

Four

Monday, June 3, 1985, 8:00 A.M.

The Juvenile Division went into overdrive the following morning, calling out the troops. Uniformed officers from the Second District were sent door-to-door through the complex. The Rescue Division dragged the canal. Later the parish drainage department even emptied the canal to facilitate the search efforts. The Sheriff's Mounted Patrol checked the nearby woods, while a helicopter checked the entire Terrytown area.

A nationwide police teletype with a revised description was sent to all law enforcement agencies in the U.S. It read:

To: All stations
FROM: Jefferson Parish Sheriff's Office, Louisiana.

27

Missing from Carrollwood Village, Gretna, LA. Nichole Jarrard Lopatta, W/F, 8 years of age, DOB: 12/07/76, 4'0", 63 pounds, long blonde hair (normally wears pigtails), blue eyes. Last seen wearing light blue tee-shirt, white collar, blue pleated skirt, white Dr. Scholl's sandals. Any information contact Jefferson Parish Sheriff's Office, Juvenile Division, ask for Det. Mitchell.

Authority/Chief Fields, JPSO

Arriving at the Tres Vidas Apartments around 9:30 A.M., Detective Rene Stallworth hurried to meet her supervisors in the apartment Fred Muller had secured as a command post. Rene, a twenty-nine-year-old black woman, had been assigned to the Personal Violence Section of the Detective Bureau for three years. Tall at 5'8", Rene had worn her usual attire, a blouse and skirt with her .38 caliber Smith and Wesson, four-inch barrel, model 10 revolver suspended from a shoulder rig.

At the command post, Rene met the ranking officers assembled, including Chief of Detectives Eugene Fields and Juvenile Detective Sergeant Craig Taffaro. She was immediately assigned to watch the mother. Fields, a pudgy man with a wide distinctive nose, a double chin, and white-gray hair, and Taffaro, a compactly built man with a receding hairline and a legendary temper, huddled with Rene. They told Rene they had questions about Jodee Lopatta's innocence because she did not respond appropriately in her initial contact with the Sheriff's Office. Simply, the powers-that-be at the Sheriff's Office felt Jodee Lopatta was not reacting the way a mother with a child missing should react. Maybe the mother had something to do with the disappearance or knew something she was not telling them? Armed with this general assumption, Rene was sent to the Lopatta apartment to monitor the mother's behavior.

Following her supervisors into the home of the missing girl, Rene met a woman whose eyes revealed a great deal of pain and confusion. And yet, the young mother still appeared hopeful. Chain-smoking Virginia Slims cigarettes, Jodee paced back and forth across her living room. Rene spotted a look of immediate disapproval from her supervisors. Jodee was dressed in a tank top without a brassiere and short-shorts.

A good detective sometimes relies on gut reactions. Rene was convinced, from her first meeting with Jodee Lopatta, that the mother was not involved in Nichole's disappearance.

Chief Fields and Sergeant Taffaro left after more questioning of the mother. Rene sat uneasily on the sofa as Jodee moved next to her to talk.

"Nichole's gonna show up," Jodee said. "I just know it." Then Jodee closed her eyes and prayed. She prayed a great deal that morning.

Renee tried her best to become a piece of furniture, to be as unobtrusive as possible. She busied herself by making mental notes about the Lopatta apartment. It was a town house with a typical two-story layout. The downstairs consisted of a living room, a kitchen with a dining area, a bedroom where Jodee's mother Eleanor stayed, a half bath, primarily used by Eleanor. There were two bedrooms upstairs. The master bedroom was occupied by the mother, while the three girls lived in the other bedroom. There were two full baths upstairs also. The common hall was cluttered with the customary photographs taken at department stores, smiling faces of three little girls in front of fake collages of windmills, autumn scenes of orange and brown leaves as foreign to south Louisiana as a Martian landscape.

Rene found the apartment depressing. Its furniture was cheap, its colors drab. Chalk white walls were in stark contrast with the dark brown carpet and dark furniture throughout the apartment. Jodee also did not appear to be the tidiest housekeeper.

The sight of the girls' grandmother was equally depressing. Eleanor came into the living room that morning and sat on the sofa after greeting Rene. She looked pale and fragile and told Rene immediately that she felt responsible. "I was supposed to be watching the girls."

Rene felt for the old woman, who seemed even smaller than her 5'2" frame. Eleanor looked like a grandmother from a Norman Rockwell painting: wrinkled skin, gray hair dotted with streaks of darker gray. She wore brown framed glasses and told Rene she had severe asthma and a heart condition. The old woman was truly suffering.

Eleanor and Jodee answered the only question Rene needed answered. Why did Jodee ask for Louis Dufour, instead of just coming out and telling the police operator, "My little girl's missing!" Rene didn't even have to prod to get an answer. All she did was mention Louis's name and the truth came out. Simply, Jodee knew Louis, who moonlighted by spinning records at the base where Jodee worked. He was a friend. He also knew Nichole. It made perfect sense to Rene, although it remained suspicious to her supervisors.

Rene was somewhat startled, two hours after arriving, when Jodee Lopatta's eyes snapped open from another prayer session and declared, "They sent you here to watch me." There was anger in her voice, yet her eyes looked sorrowful.

"I guess you're here because they don't believe I

31

don't have anything to do with my child being missing," Jodee said. "Instead of looking for my child, they would rather suspect me." Nodding slowly, Jodee closed her eyes and went back to praying. Rene felt the hairs standing up on the back of her neck.

The hairs were still standing when Juvenile Detective Muriel Biggs arrived and began interviewing the mother. Rene learned that Jodee married a man named Van Orin Jarrard in 1973, separating in 1976 and divorcing the man in 1977. Rene watched Muriel carefully note the fact that Jarrard's last contact with Jodee was in 1980. There were two children during the marriage: Jodee Bee and Nichole. Samantha was born in 1979 during Jodee's marriage to Wolfgang Lopatta. That marriage broke up in 1984. The last Jodee had seen of her second husband was as recently as April, when he returned Samantha, whom he had taken to Tennessee in January. Muriel made note of the necessary information on Wolfgang Lopatta, a Marine Corps Gunnery Sergeant, still assigned in Tennessee, as well as the name of Wolfgang's commanding officer. Jodee and Wolfgang were still legally married.

Jodee's statement to police provided several leads. She claimed that Wolfgang had abused her physically and mentally, which resulted in her leaving him, and that seven years earlier, her first husband, Van, while under the influence of alcohol, had tried

32

to kidnap their child Jodee Bee. This had happened in California, she said, and Van had held Jodee's father at gunpoint. The incident was resolved peacefully.

As Rene watched, Detective Biggs also inquired about the mother's friends, Carline Thayer, whom Jodee had gone with to Po Folks, and Norman Gibbs, who was currently sleeping upstairs. Gibbs, a local attorney, had befriended the Lopatta family. During the interview, a sleepy-eyed Gibbs came downstairs and sat next to Jodee.

Expressing the mannerisms of a boyfriend, Gibbs eagerly gave Biggs his home address and work address, phone numbers, and other data she requested. Rene etched a description of Gibbs in her mind: white male in his mid-thirties, balding blond hair, short and pudgy, with a faint moustache. Rene also noted that Jodee did not act like Gibbs's girlfriend. At first Rene thought it was due to stress, but learned over time that Jodee had little affection, if any, for Gibbs, which made their friendship all the more curious.

After the interview, Muriel Biggs took Jodee Bee outside and interviewed the little girl. Rene remained inside but soon learned that Jodee Bee had provided some interesting and somewhat confusing information. According to Nichole's big sister, the three Lopatta girls were outside Sunday playing with their friend Pepper, and Nichole "just disappeared." A few minutes later Jodee Bee added, "The man said if I told anybody, he would kill Nichole." She described the man as white with dark curly hair and a dark beard about three inches in length. She'd seen the man before, about three weeks ago, in a green truck. Jodee Bee was so nervous that Detective Biggs had to conclude the interview.

Rene could see Jodee Bee was upset when she came back into the apartment. Earlier, she'd heard the little girl say that everyone blamed her for Nichole's disappearance. After all, Jodee Bee was left in charge of her little sisters, wasn't she? Quite a burden to place on a girl eight days shy of her eleventh birthday.

Suddenly, the Juvenile Division had several leads: the ex-husband who'd once tried to kidnap one of his daughters; the estranged husband; the curious quasi-boyfriend attorney who tried his best to act as if he was at home in a house full of people who appeared to have no affection for him; and the mysterious man in the green truck.

Rene stayed at the apartment until almost midnight. It was around then that the meticulous search of the nearby woods was completed. During the search of the woods, several National Guardsmen collapsed from the heat. As soon as Jodee was told nothing was found, she let out an expression of relief. Rene could see some confusion in the eyes of several of the reserve officers. They weren't mothers. Jodee was relieved that her daughter had not been found dead. She would soon just show up.

Rene knew one thing. The mother was not involved.

Five

Tuesday, June 4, 1985.

The Times-Picayune, the metropolitan New Orleans daily newspaper, ran a photograph of Nichole Lopatta in its West Bank edition. Beneath Nichole's smiling face was written, "Missing child," along with a brief description of what Nichole was wearing and the fact she was last seen at 4:30 P.M., on Sunday, at the Tres Vidas. According to the Jefferson Parish Sheriff's Office spokesman, Sgt. Susan Miller, "foul play is not suspected."

Tuesday brought a flurry of activity from the Juvenile Division. A composite drawing was made of the mysterious bearded man with the green truck. Listed as a possible suspect, the drawing featured a wide-faced man with black curly hair and a matching beard, a wide nose and wide set eyes. He was described as a white male, six feet tall with a pot-belly.

Sergeant Norman Schultz, a quiet, efficient veteran with a meticulous method of taking things one step at a time, took control of the Juvenile Division's investigation. Schultz, nearing forty, with sandy blond hair, looked like a cop: clean shaven, neat haircut, white shirt and tie. He immediately made sure the FBI was contacted and asked to assist in the investigation. Although many local policemen distrust the FBI, which had been accused in the past of hogging headlines and elbowing detectives out of the way because they are "the big boys"; good investigators, like Schultz, knew better. The FBI not only had the resources, but some extremely able investigators and were specialists in investigating kidnappings. Why not use the best tools available? Schultz wasn't worried about headlines. A little girl was *missing*.

Schultz reinterviewed Jodee Bee and found some additions to the story given to Detective Biggs. Apparently, on Saturday, the day before Nichole disappeared, at about 4:30 P.M., Jodee Bee, Nichole, and little sister Samantha were sitting on a bench at the Tres Vidas, near apartment 100. The man from the composite drawing came out between apartments 85 and 86, approached, and stopped next to Nichole. The man gave Nichole a bag of candy and

37

said, "I'll see you on Sunday." The man was wearing a white shirt with short sleeves and blue jeans. Other children came forward corroborating Jodee Bee's story.

Another child, around Nichole's age, was certain he saw Nichole at the Tres Vidas swimming pool between 5:30 and 6:30 P.M., on Sunday. Nichole was sitting and talking to a slender man in blue jeans.

Still another youth reported that Nichole was positively at Cowboy's Deli at the corner of Behrman Highway and Carol Sue Boulevard in Gretna, at 3:30 P.M., on Sunday.

Another resident of the Tres Vidas informed the Jefferson Parish Sheriff's Office that she *definitely* saw Nichole Lopatta on *Monday*, around 7:30 A.M. Nichole was "just standing" and looking ahead, like "she were a zombie."

Several children presented a story that a man, fitting the same description as the man in the composite, and driving a green truck, exposed himself to the children, also on Saturday, June 1.

Detectives scrambled, rousing several white males with past sex offenses on their rap sheets. A man in nearby Harvey, Louisiana, was checked out by Rene Stallworth. A man in Westwego, Louisiana, was interviewed by detectives. After enough known or suspected sex offenders were located, a photographic lineup was compiled and shown to the children of the Tres Vidas. None of the suspects was identified as the man with the green truck.

The FBI began their investigation by interviewing friends of the Lopatta family, including Carline Thayer. They secured a list of bars that Jodee Lopatta frequented: The CPO Club at the Naval Supply Station in New Orleans, Port of Call on Dauphine Street, Chevy's on Tchoupitoulas Street, and The Park in Metairie. They also secured the names of several men who were friends of Jodee: Mark (last name unknown) who was a bartender at the CPO Club; Arthur (last name unknown) also from the CPO Club; a navy lieutenant named Jerry Perez; a man named Peter from Texas; "Big Lou" who was described as a disc jockey at the CPO Club and later identified as Louis Dufour; as well as local attorney Norman Gibbs, the man who was at the Lopatta house when Rene Stallworth arrived on Monday, June 3.

Gibbs was described as "strange" by several friends of the Lopattas. He was overly friendly, especially to the children. Eleanor Mallory told Rene Stallworth as much, labeling Gibbs as "a touch feminine." According to the old woman, Jodee had asked Gibbs not to come around the previous Wednesday. Eleanor also stated that Gibbs was closest to Nichole, of all the children. Curious, because

Rene noted little sadness or remorse in Gibbs that Monday.

A neighbor of the Lopattas volunteered a bothersome insight into the family. Noting his own stepdaughter had been a subject of sexual abuse, the man stated that Nichole displayed some of the same traits: fear of being alone, a laid-back attitude to life. Neighbors described Jodee Lopatta as "strange" and an "uncaring" mother who allowed her children to run around the complex.

Rene was back in the Lopatta apartment Tuesday evening when Detective Judy Long arrived with, of all things, a psychic. Judy Long, an attractive young detective with a tenacious curiosity, was disarming in her beauty. *Too good-looking to be a cop* was the common thought among her fellow road deputies, back when Judy was a rookie. Many of them took it upon themselves to be overprotective of this petite woman, who looked smaller in her dark blue uniform. It didn't take much time for Judy to prove she didn't need protection. Judy was as feisty as she was pretty, and far smarter than most of the men trying to mother her.

Around 8:30 P.M., Judy showed up at the Lopatta apartment with a woman named Donna Bray from Picayune, Mississippi. Like Judy, Donna had long, brown hair. Shorter and heavier in stature, Donna wore clothes that Rene could only describe as eccentric. Adorned in a flowing dress and scarves of various shades of green and earth tones, Donna's entrance was wrought with drama. Rene felt a "piercing aura" around the woman as soon as she entered. She commanded attention.

Meeting Jodee Lopatta, Donna immediately extended emotional support to the young mother. She advised everyone to allow Jodee room to "breathe," to give the young mother support.

Donna went to Nichole's room with Judy. Rene remained in the hallway. Requesting absolute silence, Donna concentrated. Judy was not even allowed to take written notes as Donna moved around and touched Nichole's bed, the little girl's clothes and toys, lingering on a stuffed animal. A moment later, Donna clutched her chest and gasped loudly.

"Your child is in extreme pain," Donna told Jodee. She also claimed that more than one spirit was involved. One of the persons involved in the abduction was not connected to the others, who were closely connected spirits. Donna described green-colored towers, an interstate highway, and a nearby waterway. Donna then announced she was ready to go and left. She didn't even socialize.

Rene ran the leads through her mind: green-colored towers, an interstate highway, a nearby waterway. Louisiana was dotted with green electrical towers all along its only interstate, Interstate 10, which crossed about a hundred waterways from the Pearl River border with Mississippi through the backwaters of Lake Charles, all the way to Orange, Texas. That narrowed things, of course. According to the psychic, Nichole was not in Arizona or Mexico. She was somewhere in south Louisiana, and in "extreme pain."

Six

Wednesday, June 5, 1985.

The Times-Picayune ran an article entitled "Wooded area searched for child," which reported that hundreds of sheriff's deputies, FBI agents, military personnel, and volunteers had searched a wooded area in Terrytown, for missing Nichole Lopatta. Quoting unnamed officials, the paper reported that Nichole was last seen about 7:00 or 8:00 P.M., Sunday, at a convenience store on Behrman Highway. The paper also claimed there was another report that Nichole was seen going into some woods where neighborhood children frequently played.

"It's just a good cooperative spirit," FBI Agent Wayne Taylor was quoted. "It's an obvious show of care and concern on a very warm day."

Wednesday was another stifling day in New Orleans. A relentless heat wave had descended on the

43

city, occasionally relieved by sudden semitropical rainstorms that dumped inches of water in a matter of minutes, before moving on.

The command post was a beehive of activity. With the release to the media of the composite drawing of the mysterious bearded man with the green truck, calls began coming in by the dozens.

While special agents of the FBI verified the whereabouts and the alibi for Wolfgang Friedrich Lopatta in Tennessee, special agents from the New Orleans FBI field office continued on their interviews at the Tres Vidas. Speaking to residents, including several little girls, the FBI attempted to piece together the last known movements of Nichole Lopatta. Many of the children had seen Nichole on Sunday; had played with Nichole. It did not take long for investigators to realize that every time they spoke to Jodee Bee and the other children around the complex, they got a different story. One child saw Nichole playing "with worms" by the Coke machine, while another said Nichole was playing with some black children. One woman reported that Nichole had an argument with her mother over adopting a kitten the preceding Wednesday.

A frightened neighbor came forward with the story that her daughter, about two weeks previously, had come home and said someone had showed her his "Tu Tu." The neighbor thought her daughter was talking about another child, until the victim's disappearance. When finally questioned by police, the daughter didn't even remember the incident.

Returning from following up a bogus lead in nearby Harvey, Louisiana, Rene heard the stories at the command post about Nichole sightings and mysterious men. One story of interest involved Norman Gibbs. He was apparently seen correcting Nichole recently when she had dug up some worms. After making Nichole drop the worms, Gibbs gave her, "three small slaps on the buttocks." Then Gibbs hugged her.

Throughout the day, it became apparent that Norman Gibbs was beginning to emerge as a possible suspect. No matter who was interviewed, everyone said that Gibbs was particularly fond of Nichole, and *he*, like Nichole's mother, was not displaying enough emotion about the disappearance.

The calls to the command post came fast and without respite. A schoolteacher at a nearby school fit the composite. That man proved to be guilty of nothing, except an accidental resemblance to the now infamous composite.

Detectives were called to a large shopping center by security guards because a man fitting the description was "acting suspiciously." That man turned out to be a teenager.

A man fitting the description of the composite

was seen at a convenience store. He too was "acting suspiciously." So was another man at a McDonald's in Metairie. Both were gone before the police arrived.

Green pickup trucks were stopped all over the metro area and drivers checked out.

The investigators received a call from the police in Biloxi, Mississippi, volunteering the name and a mug shot of one of their sex criminals, who actually lived in Denham Springs, Louisiana, about sixty miles from New Orleans. Although he drove a red Firebird, he fit the composite. The Gulfport Police checked out a subject fitting the composite in a 7-Eleven Store.

The St. Bernard Parish Sheriff's Office, south of New Orleans, provided the names of twin males, who fit the composite.

A host of names were given to investigators by concerned citizens. "The composite looks like . . . ," a frantic voice would say, and another name was added to the list of those to be investigated.

One man demanded investigators look into a suspicious man who had followed his wife home four months earlier. The man could provide only one piece of information. The man drove a brown car.

As detectives logged each call and set up plans to follow up each lead, a twenty-five-year-old black man arrived at the Tres Vidas Apartments Office and asked for the names and phone numbers of the white women who lived there. When his request was denied, he bluntly said he needed the names because he wanted to rape and kill the women there. The man was quickly arrested and taken to the psychiatric ward of Charity Hospital in New Orleans, where deputies learned the man had been released from the same ward, after a two-week stay, that very morning.

A reporter from the Channel Six television station called to volunteer the name of someone who fit the description and drove a brown pickup.

Later, at 6:25 P.M., New Orleans police pulled over a man fitting the composite. That man turned out to be a Channel Eight television cameraman.

A total of fifty-two calls with leads were received at the command post on Wednesday. Information was gathered on potential suspects as far away as Arizona.

An excited United Cab driver called to say he'd picked up a man who fit the description in New Orleans's French Quarter, at the corner of Bourbon and Toulouse Streets, and drove the man to New Orleans International Airport. "The man was definitely *gay*."

"Did he leave on a plane?" a weary investigator

asked.

"Sure."

"What airline?"

"I don't know."

"What was his destination?"

"I don't know."

The investigator thanked the caller and hung up.

Several women called to turn in men they knew who had "problems with flashing." These names were logged down, too.

FBI Special Agent Linda Harrison came on some disquieting information that evening. A neighborhood girl, Nichole's age, relayed a story of molestation involving Nichole. Some weeks earlier she and Nichole were playing by the Tres Vidas pool when a man approached, took the girls by the hand, brought them to the Lopatta apartment where he removed both girls' clothes, except their panties, and then his own clothes, except his underwear. The man kissed both girls on the lips, and stuck his tongue in their mouths. He touched them "all over." This was followed by more intimate touching, which involved cunnilingus and masturbation.

Afterward the man took the little girls to a convenience store, where he bought them candy and bubble gum. The man drove a green pickup. Although the little girl did not know the man's name, she said she'd seen him by the Lopatta apartment

48

before.

Even later, Special Agent Harrison secured a statement from a four-year-old Tres Vidas girl who relayed another story of molestation involving a white male who approached her at the Tres Vidas swimming pool.

Things were heating up.

Seven

Thursday, June 6, 1985.

A photo of Jodee Lopatta in horn-rimmed sunglasses was prominently displayed in the morning edition of *The Times-Picayune*. She was talking to an FBI agent "near the search site." The accompanying article was entitled "Hundreds comb woods, but find no trace of girl." Nichole's picture was also displayed, that same shy smile on her young face. Next to Nichole's picture was a drawing of the area around the Tres Vidas, "Missing child search area." The article detailed the search by nearly three hundred people for Nichole, centered on the densely wooded area near the Tres Vidas.

The paper also ran a picture of the composite of the mysterious man with the green pickup, describing the man as around forty with curly hair and a beard. On their way to work, the juvenile detectives mentally prepared themselves to be inundated with calls.

* * *

Attorney Norman Gibbs was interviewed by FBI Special Agent Jack Johnston and Jefferson Parish Detective David Phillips in his Metairie apartment. He was friendly and seemed eager to answer the lawmen's questions. He did not seem to understand at that time that he was emerging as the prime suspect in the disappearance of Nichole.

Sitting on his living room sofa, Gibbs claimed to have known Jodee Lopatta for about three months. He had met her at her place of employment, the Navy Station. He described their relationship as social.

"Is this a sexual relationship?" Gibbs was asked.

"No," Gibbs answered. "First, I wouldn't do it at her place, with the children there. It isn't proper. Second, Mrs. Lopatta is still legally married."

Gibbs went on to state that at times the Lopatta girls called him "uncle," and he always corrected them.

"Has Jodee Lopatta or any of the children ever been to your apartment?"

"No," Gibbs answered.

"Were the girls friendly to you?"

Gibbs said yes, absolutely. Nichole most of all. "She's my favorite."

"Have you ever been alone with the girls?"

51

"Sure. Shopping, to the fair, to the grocery, to get ice cream."

The investigators then asked Gibbs what he had done on Sunday. He detailed his activities without a problem. He was a lawyer and knew what they were doing. They were getting him on the record, checking out his alibi.

After putting in a few hours alone in his office Sunday morning, Gibbs returned home after 11:00 A.M., and called Jodee Lopatta. Nichole answered and said her mommy wasn't there. Gibbs did some laundry, then watched an NBA basketball game on TV. He called Jodee back around 4:00 P.M. Jodee was on the other line and said she'd call him back. She did, sometime between 6:00 and 6:30 P.M. While on the phone with Gibbs, Jodee Bee started talking to her mother, at which time Jodee asked her daughter, "Where's Nichole?"

"I don't know," Jodee Bee answered.

Jodee then told Gibbs she'd have to get off the line to go look for Nichole. Around 7:00 P.M., Jodee called Gibbs back and sounded upset. She couldn't find Nichole. Gibbs drove over and helped search for Nichole as soon as he arrived at the Tres Vidas.

Originally from Cleveland, Gibbs was asked some blunt questions. He had no problem with them, denying he had no criminal record. Gibbs said he had never approached the Lopatta children in a sexual manner, nor had he molested the children.

Gibbs was polite and never displayed any discomfort during the questioning. To investigators, he was either an innocent man, or a stone-cold liar.

Forty-seven-year-old Conerly Mizell didn't read the morning paper. He knew nothing of Nichole Lopatta, or the search for the little girl. He never saw the composite drawing. Parking his pickup alongside U.S. Highway 51, in rural St. John The Baptist Parish, Louisiana, Conerly grabbed his new binoculars and walked into the woods off the road.

Glancing around the heavily wooded area, Conerly adjusted the focus on his binoculars. Satisfied with their clarity, he continued his walk, checking out trees in the distance. About one hundred feet into the woods, along a narrow footpath, Conerly smelled something. He thought it was garbage at first. He took in a deep breath and nearly gagged. Whatever it was, it was dead.

Peering through the weeds, about ten feet from the footpath, Conerly saw it and retched. Stumbling back, he hurried out of the woods, gagging as he moved. Standing alongside the highway, he looked around at the empty road for a moment before tossing his binoculars into the cab of his truck and climbing in.

Louisiana State Troopers Edgar Clay and Clennard Ross had just finished talking and were maneuvering their respective police cars around to leave the parking lot of the Holiday Inn on U.S. 51 in La Place, Louisiana, when a pickup hurried into the lot and sped up to them. The driver, a middle-aged black man, waved frantically at them. Ross, whose car was in front, rolled his window down. The black man climbed out and stepped up to the police car.

"Officer, I found a body."

"What kind of body?" Ross wasn't being sarcastic, though he knew it sounded that way.

"I'm not sure. Could be a big animal. But I think it's human."

"Where?"

"About four miles up the road. It's in the woods."

"You're gonna have to show us," Ross advised.

"Sure." Conerly shrugged. He looked as if he was waiting to see which car he would ride in, when Ross told him he'd better take his truck. "If it's human, we're gonna have to stay there a while."

"Okay."

On the way, Trooper Clay called his headquarters on the radio, notifying LSP Troop B what the officers were up to.

Approximately four miles later, after slowing down several times, seemingly unsure of the location, Mizell finally parked alongside the highway. The troopers followed the man into the woods. Clay noticed a piece of carpet hanging in a small tree as they entered the woods. *Good landmark,* he thought to himself.

One hundred feet into the woods the black man stopped and pointed ahead and to their right. Trooper Ross stopped and took the time to secure the name of their escort. Clay moved forward, immediately encountering a foul stench. Spotting the source, he inched closer and took long seconds to study the grotesque sight in front of him. He'd stopped about ten feet from the nude, badly decomposed body of a female lying on its left side in a slight curl. He noted that its head was pointed in a northerly direction. That was for his report. He noted the road behind him was east of the location and traveled north.

Clay made other mental notes. The flesh was so dark he couldn't tell the race of the body. He could tell it was burnt, lying under a blistering Louisiana sun. The body was also swollen, bloated to an obscene degree. Clay noted its brownish blond hair was separated from its skull about eight to twelve inches.

Withdrawing from the stench, Clay radioed headquarters. He reported that they had found the decomposed body of a female, about thirteen years of age. He surmised that the body had been in the woods from two weeks to a month.

Now it was time to wait. The Sheriff's Office would have to handle this. State troopers in Louisiana were highway patrolmen. Specialists in traffic control and accidents, the only bodies they handled were accident victims. *This was probably a homicide,* the trooper surmised.

At 2:31 P.M., Operator Argie Clement of the St. John The Baptist Parish Sheriff's Office communication center received a call from Troop B, advising of a Signal 29 (death), about five miles north of the Interstate-10 overpass on U.S. 51 in La Place. Clement immediately called for detectives.

Both Clay and Ross were tempted to wait back on the road. They stepped away from the body, only to discover that the smell stayed with them. It was on their uniforms.

While waiting, Clay stepped back to the body and trained his policeman eyes on the scene. He noticed several articles that seemed out of place in the area, most noteworthy a *Penthouse* magazine that seemed undisturbed by the weather. On its cover was the title of a curious article. It read, "I killed 350 people."

The magazine was located about ten feet east of the body. Clay also observed two white handkerchiefs near the body, a third a few inches farther. All appeared fairly clean. Troopers Berry and Favor arrived on the scene to help secure it until the detectives arrived.

At 2:37 P.M., Detective Sergeant Robert Hay arrived. Still in his twenties, Hay, known to friends as "Bobby," spoke in a Cajun accent common to south Louisiana. He was having a nightmarish day. Earlier he had handled the recovery of another body, not two miles away. Positively a murder victim, Hay's first body of the day was a white male in his mid-twenties, about six feet tall, with brown hair and eighty-four stab wounds. Its left hand had been severed and its right hand partially severed. *Yes, it had been a helluva day already.*

Before entering the woods, Hay questioned Trooper Ross. Accompanied by Chief of Detectives Joseph Oubre, who'd arrived a few seconds earlier, Hay was led to the body.

An experienced professional, Hay took meticulous notes as he carefully processed the crime scene. He measured the distance from the west shoulder of U.S. Highway 51 down the footpath that led to the body. It measured 146.9 feet. The body was exactly twenty feet from the footpath. He noted that the body appeared to be that of a small nude white female, possessing a foul stench, and covered with maggots and insects. Decomposed, the skin was turning brown and black in some areas, common under the strong summer sun. Hay described the hair as long and blond in color. Most of the scalp hair lay on the ground away from the head. The body's left arm was extended outward in a southerly direction, its palm facing up. The legs were bent with the right leg on top of the left. The body was bloated. The head and facial area was covered with what appeared to be a dark cloth or material. Hay noted that it might have been wrapped around the head. Hay then measured the distances between the body and the nearest canal. It measured 169.2 feet. In his notes he also jotted the fact that the footpath was frequently traveled by fishermen and was used to dump garbage in the past.

Moving back to the highway, Hay called his headquarters to request a crime lab technician from the nearby Jefferson Parish Sheriff's Office Crime Lab, which often assisted smaller parishes with important crime scene processing. Hay also asked for St. John Sheriff's Officer Mike Segur to come and videotape the crime scene. Then Hay questioned Conerly Mizell himself.

Continually wiping perspiration from his brow

Hay learned how the body came to be found. The temperature was well into the high nineties with matching high humidity. Conerly Mizell, also sweating under the blistering sun, confirmed that he had seen no one else in the woods around the time he'd discovered the body.

When the assistant coroner, Dr. Collin Bailey, arrived at 3:40 P.M., Hay escorted him to the body, which was then pronounced "dead." The cause of death was listed as "undetermined" pending autopsy.

Jefferson Parish Crime Scene Technician Bill Viera arrived shortly before four o'clock. He waited as Mike Segur videotaped the scene before moving in to take photographs. Then Viera and Hay secured physical evidence:

1. Two pieces of brown cardboard with unknown red dried stains and unknown white stains.
2. Three white cloth handkerchiefs (balled up).
3. Three paper napkins (balled up).
4. Two magazines (one with a story about Henry Lee Lucas).
5. One piece of cotton shirt (yellow) with multicolored stripes.

6. One white cotton T-shirt (Fruit of the Loom brand).
7. One white towel with "Property of Mount Sinai" stenciled in brown on its front.

The body was removed at five o'clock by Earl Baloney and Carl King, ambulance attendants of Baloney's Ambulance Service. It was transported to the Orleans Parish Coroner's Office in the basement of the Criminal Courts Building, at the corner of Tulane Avenue and Broad Avenue, in downtown New Orleans.

Remaining officers conducted another canvass of the entire area for any more physical evidence, to no avail. After obtaining over-view photographs from the elevated portion of nearby I-55, Viera and Segur left.

Most of their concentration centered around the magazine with the article about Henry Lee Lucas. Allegedly, the most prolific serial killer in U.S. history, Lucas was capturing headlines across the country with admissions of killing hundreds of women. His travels had taken Lucas through south Louisiana. In fact, Lucas had admitted murdering women in Jefferson and Orleans Parishes, among others.

Sergeant Hay left shortly before six o'clock, his nostrils still smelling decomposed flesh, his shirt dripping with perspiration. He thought to himself what he wouldn't say aloud. He thought of the words no one in St. John ever said aloud . . . *dumping ground*. That's what St. John and St. Charles Parishes were becoming. They were dumping grounds for bodies that almost always came from one of America's most violent cities, that beautiful lady down river called New Orleans.

In New Orleans, FBI special agents interviewed a little girl neighbor of Nichole Lopatta, one who had seen Nichole walk off with a white male on Sunday. The FBI showed the girl a photographic lineup, consisting of eight pictures. The girl picked out #6, as the man who had been seen walking away with Nichole on Sunday at about 7:00 P.M. She said that "the man had very strange eyes."

The man, whose photograph was actually a police mug shot, was well-known to Jefferson Parish detectives, because of his trouble-making family. Originally from Barataria and Lafitte, fishing villages in south Jefferson Parish, the family bragged that they were descended from pirates (Jean Lafitte's Barataria Bay Pirates). Over the years more than one had been arrested for murder, rape, robbery, and various drug charges.

The FBI and Jefferson Parish detectives now had

61

another reason to roust them.

At the St. John The Baptist Parish Sheriff's Office station, Hay sent out a nationwide call requesting information on missing young females. He did his best to describe the clothing draped over the body, but the colors were unclear due to exposure to the elements and body fluids.

Hay busied himself writing two daily reports, one for each of the bodies found on a day no one would easily forget in sleepy St. John Parish.

Detective Barry Wood of the Jefferson Parish Sheriff's Office Homicide Unit, on his way to work the evening watch, avoided the usual traffic jam on the Greater New Orleans Mississippi River Bridge by staying on the east bank of the river as long as possible. At 6:30 P.M., with the strong sun still up in the western sky, still heating up the city, Wood accessed Interstate 10 and headed through traffic toward the West Bank. *The bridge shouldn't be as crowded after six,* Wood thought. *Unless some asshole had run into the back of some other asshole on the fuckin' bridge.* Until a second span could be completed adjacent to the existing bridge, the GNOMRB was better known as the Greater New Orleans Mississippi River Bridge Parking Lot.

Barry Wood, a tall, lanky man with short dark

hair and a full moustache, best described as a cross between actors Dennis Weaver and Sam Elliot, was known to his partners as "Country-ass." Back working Homicide after a year's hiatus as a private investigator, Wood didn't have much of a case load and was happy to be that way. As a veteran homicide dick, he knew it wouldn't last. But it beat PI work. A year as a slimy civilian PI was more than Wood could handle. Asked to lie repeatedly and to cheat people by the cream of the New Orleans legal community, Wood was glad to be rid of working for lawyers who would call to give an assignment, beginning a case with, "First of all, this call never occurred."

While still on I-10, Wood heard his sergeant, Robert Masson, calling him on the police radio, Wood knew he was about to be nailed. Masson, an ace supervisor with a monotone radio voice, asked Wood to proceed to the Orleans Parish Coroner's Office to attend a postmortem on the body from St. John Parish. The body, in an advanced state of decomposition, was unidentified. Wood responded in the affirmative.

Jesus, he thought to himself. Bad enough to attend an autopsy of one of their own "stinkers," but Wood didn't relish sitting in on one from St. John Parish until Masson came back on the air with the kicker. The body was that of a young, white female.

Wood could read between the lines. A body found in a rural parish had to be connected to something big or he wouldn't be sent. The name Nichole Lopatta came to mind immediately.

Entering the garage along the South White Street side of the Criminal Courts Building at Tulane and Broad, Wood smelled something familiar to a homicide man who'd spent many long hours witnessing autopsies. He smelled decay. He was glad he'd worn a cheap sport coat and dress pants, instead of a nice suit that day. Getting that smell out of your clothes took more than one trip to the cleaners.

The Orleans Parish morgue occupied Room 101 in the garage beneath a building that housed the New Orleans criminal district courts. A concrete mass of a building, this large gray hulk was built during the Works Progress Administration, after the Great Depression. Forbidding and cold, the large building had all the charm of a castle dungeon.

It was unusual for Wood, to be at the coroner's office for an autopsy in the evening. Autopsies started at 8:00 A.M., and finished when the bodies stacked in the hall were done.

Wood entered the morgue's timeworn wooden door and walked down the hall, past the refrigeration units, which were always full. Wood met the pathologist, Dr. Paul McGarry, in the hall, along with two Jefferson juvenile detectives who were armed with a photo of Nichole Lopatta. Also present was Detective Sergeant Kenneth Mitchell from St. John Parish. The men exchanged nods and followed the pathologist into the autopsy room.

McGarry, a small man with a balding head ringed with hair around his ears and along the back of his head, reminded Wood of the Jerry Lewis character, The Nutty Professor. McGarry was a very quiet man, one a detective didn't ask questions of prior to his initial examination of a body, unless McGarry initiated the questioning.

Resembling a laboratory from a bad *Frankenstein* movie, the autopsy room consisted of two metal tables surrounded by shelves which held an assortment of glass containers filled with different colored liquid substances and God only knew what else. The Orleans Parish Morgue, commonly called "The Chamber of Horrors," had more in common with a medieval torture chamber than a modern forensic laboratory. Poorly ventilated, damp and cold even on the hottest day of the year, it always reeked of death.

Lying on one of the stainless steel tables was the bloated body of a young female. Wood turned back to the juvenile detectives and said, "You can put the picture away."

The body had no face. Its flesh had been eaten away, down to the bone. Wood recognized the unmistakable marks of animal and insect bites on the face. Maggots were present on the body, around the face and head, around the chest and vaginal area.

Jesus! Nice way to spend an evening, Wood thought to himself. *Doing another parish's work for them. Not like Jefferson Parish didn't have enough murders of its own.*

No facial features were left on the body. Her eyes were gone, and only the exposed jaws and teeth revealed this to be a child. Her honey-colored hair was barely attached to the skullcap.

Who was she? Wood thought. His mind began to work, tugging at him with questions, causing him to wonder what this girl had been like. Did she play with dolls like most little girls? Did she run under a strong sun, like a tomboy, laughing and joking? Did she jump rope? Did she make mud pies? Did she ride her bicycle with her friends, her long hair streaming behind? Did she even own a bicycle? Or was she a child so abused on this earth, a child whose entire life was a nightmare that death finally ended? *Whoever she was,* Wood realized as he withdrew from the table, *she suffered a death so terrible that it could only be described, as it inevitably would be described, in the cold description of a police report.*

66

Experienced enough at observing the leftovers of violent death, Wood knew that tissue damaged prior to death was more susceptible to decomposition. The girl's battered face, chest, and vaginal area told Wood how horrible her death must have been.

Juvenile Detective Muriel Biggs took out the picture of Nichole Lopatta, stood next to the head of the body and declared, "That's her. Look at the bone structure."

Wood wasn't so sure. The body was awfully big. Then again, he knew how a body could bloat to nearly twice its size under a persistent sun as the gases inside expanded.

However, Dr. McGarry did not like anyone asking him questions or giving him information that he did not request. He did not like to be told about his victims by officers whose information may temper his objective observations of the cadaver.

With Muriel Biggs hovering over the body, Wood could see she was treading on thin ice. On several occasions McGarry shot Biggs a stern look as she bantered around the autopsy table.

Wood remained out of the way. Standing with his back against the wall, Wood watched Jefferson Parish fingerprint expert Merril Boling step up to secure fingerprints from the body. Boling, retired from the New Orleans Police Department, took pride in his work and relished catching idiot criminals stupid enough to leave latent prints at the crime scene.

A chubby fellow with a round face, Boling reminded Wood of a department store Santa Claus, except Boling's curly, brown hair showed only a hint of gray. As usual, Boling had a cigar in his mouth, one of those especially stinky cheap stogies. Once a detective complained about the odor, and Boling quipped that his cigars were handpicked by growers who had observed dogs pissing on the tobacco leaves. On this day, Wood was happy to see the cigar lit in Boling's mouth. Anything to diminish the sharp smell of decay.

Although Boling was good, he had trouble fingerprinting the small fingers of the body. The flesh kept slipping. But he managed to get good prints of the victim's right and left thumbs.

Boling quickly left to return to Jefferson Parish to compare the prints to fingerprints Jodee Lopatta had taken of Nichole and her sisters back when they lived in Tennessee. There was a police sponsored fingerprint program to help parents identify their children, in the event of kidnapping or death.

Wood was thinking about that as Boling left, thinking about a country where such programs were becoming commonplace, thinking about witnessing the autopsy of a little girl, which was also becoming

. . . commonplace.

Watching the pathologist conduct a preliminary examination, Wood noted the following, as dictated by Dr. McGarry:

White Female
Age: 11 to 12 years (approximate)
4'5" to 4'5½" long
60 to 70 pounds in weight (alive)
Dark blond hair, 12" to 14" in length, wavy at the ends
Short fingernails, pink polish on nails

Not content that the body would be quickly identified, Wood requested fingernail polish scrapings from the little girl's nails, as well as soil samples and hair samples.

While this was being done by the crime lab technician, Wood learned of the other body that had been recovered in St. John that morning, the young white male with the missing hand and the eighty-four stab wounds.

"Have to be connected," Wood said aloud.

No one asked why. But a good homicide man didn't believe in coincidences.

As Dr. McGarry spoke into his recorder, Wood

took note that the body was found with one piece of clothing on it, a sleeveless collared pullover blouse, so saturated with body fluids, its color was obscured. Wood discovered, on closer examination, that a small piece of the blouse that wasn't wet was light blue in color. He also noted small flowers embroidered on the blouse. The blouse was a size twelve, Sears brand.

McGarry felt the victim had been dead about five days to a week. Nichole had been missing four days. Close enough for Wood. McGarry's examination revealed that, whoever this young girl had been, she had suffered terribly. There was trauma to her vagina prior to death. The body had also been sexually molested annally. Her jaw was broken. At least three upper front teeth were missing and appeared to have been knocked out by a blow.

McGarry postponed the complete autopsy until the following morning when he could have assistance from another pathologist or coroner's investigator.

Wood and the Jefferson detectives departed with their evidence and information. Arriving at the Jefferson Parish Crime Lab in Metairie, Wood turned over the evidence to Technician Carol Dixon. Discussing the case with Dixon, they agreed that securing maggots from the body would be important. Maggots have a definite incubation period; determine the maturity of the maggots and you have a pretty solid date of death. They agreed that maggots should be collected from the different areas of the body.

Wood and Dixon returned to "The Chamber of Horrors," and convinced a lone morgue attendant to allow them to secure the maggots from three different areas of the body.

Back at the crime lab, Wood learned that Merril Boling had positively identified the body as that of Nichole Lopatta, age eight. Boling and FBI Special Agents Freddy Cleveland and Robert Turkavage, fingerprint experts, had studied the prints taken at the morgue carefully, comparing them to the prints supplied by Jodee Lopatta. The thumbprints were conclusive.

It was after 12:30 A.M. by then and Wood thought, *Why didn't they contact us sooner about the identification?* He and Dixon and Crime Lab Director Ron Singer were well on their way in analyzing the maggots for growth time.

Later, he discovered that the chiefs had decided to question the mother immediately after the identification and never bothered contacting Wood or the crime lab. At least Wood wouldn't have to attend the complete autopsy in the morning. Masson advised that another detective, Steve Buras from the day watch, would handle it.

Wood was more than weary. Driving home at 1:00 A.M., he had a lot to think about. A typical homicide dick who'd never shot anyone, Wood sat heavily in the recliner of his living room, in darkness, and thought how much he'd *love* to shoot the cocksucker who did this. But this case wasn't his problem. It was St. John's problem. There had been a kidnapping of a juvenile in Jefferson Parish, a crime handled by the Juvenile Division. The murder belonged to St. John. Wood thanked God.

With the Juvenile Division handling the initial investigation, Wood was certain it was handled improperly. The first forty-eight hours of a homicide investigation were the most important. Juvenile detectives, following their historical method of suspecting the victim's family and friends, rarely stayed with the facts when investigating. They usually made quick observations and then jumped to a general conclusion.

The Juvenile Division, geared for a missing person case, was in no way capable of handling a criminal homicide investigation. People were questioned quickly to ascertain if they had seen the child, not where they were at the time or whom they were with. Wood was certain a lot of backtracking would have to be done, a lot of gaps to be filled.

Already, Wood had heard several stories that had come from the children of the area, stories that continually changed, continually evolved as a child's imagination would normally evolve. He knew a child's imagination was a wondrous thing, but a nightmare when it came to the reality of a homicide investigation.

This was one case Wood was glad he wouldn't have to handle.

He had no idea how wrong he was.

Eight

Friday, June 7, 1985.

The Times-Picayune ran a lead article entitled "Girl strangled, autopsy shows." While authorities searched the swampy area around Interstate 10 in St. John Parish, where Nichole's body had been found, along with the body of an unidentified man (less than two miles apart), the coroner's office reported its preliminary examination revealed Nichole had been strangled.

According to Sheriff's Office spokesperson, Judi Guillory, Nichole had been found, ". . . clothed only in her shirt and it was pulled over her head. There was no face left. It was horrible, absolutely horrible."

The unidentified dead man with the missing hand was also reported found nude. The man was described as being in his mid-twenties with medium-length, brown hair, 6' to 6'2" tall, weighing about

180 pounds with a tattoo on his upper left arm of a skull and crossbones, the initials "USMC" and the name "Billy." The coroner listed his cause of death as drowning, although his left hand had been sawed off, his right hand partially sawed off, and he had suffered partial castration.

The paper quoted one Tres Vidas resident who said, "I'm keeping my children inside until we find out what happened."

Jefferson Parish Sheriff Harry Lee confirmed that a psychic had been used to try to hunt down the killer. Lee claimed the psychic knew details about the case that had not been made public.

"You can call it Hocus-pocus," Lee said, "but it can't hurt us to try."

In a supporting article, *The Times-Picayune* detailed how Jodee Lopatta was told at 11:00 P.M., the previous evening, of the positive identification of her daughter's body, how she fainted and had to be carried to her sofa by friends. The paper went on to chronicle Jodee's last day of her vigil, climaxing with how a bill collector visited her because she was late with her rent, and how a sheriff's deputy followed a short while later with an eviction notice. The paper even had quotes as to Jodee's emotional response and how the "sheepish" deputy quietly left.

Detective Barry Wood read the articles with his

75

morning coffee and was sickened at the growing American thirst for all the lurid "true crime" news.

At 9:00 A.M., an associate of Attorney Norman Gibbs reported to the Jefferson Parish Sheriff's Office that he suspected Gibbs was involved in the Nichole Lopatta kidnapping and murder.

Samuel Dillon, a twenty-nine-year-old white male, said that Gibbs had been a "wallflower" all week since Nichole was missing. Dillon could not understand how Gibbs could be so close to the Lopatta family and show no emotion.

Dillon also said he didn't like that fact that Nichole would climb into Gibb's lap during Gibb's frequent visits to the Lopatta apartment. Jodee apparently did not want Gibbs to be close to her children, but he was anyway. Gibbs acted as if he was at home at the Lopatta house.

Recently rejected by Jodee, Gibbs was "upset." Dillon said he thought Jodee tolerated Gibbs because of his relationship with her children.

Dillon had no direct information linking Gibbs to Nichole's disappearance or murder. He just "felt" the things he reported and thought he should share them with the police.

The autopsy of Nichole Lopatta was completed on the morning of June 7 by Dr. Paul A. McGarry of the Orleans Parish Coroner's Office at the request of Dr. S.J. St. Martin, Coroner of St. John The Baptist Parish.

In addition to his previously reported observations, the pathologist noted that the upper canine tooth was missing, as well as the lower canine teeth. There was a fracture through the mandible between the right lateral incisor tooth and the canine, "completely through." Nichole's jaw had been broken in two.

The doctor listed his provisional autopsy diagnoses:

1. Recent head injury, fractured skull, fractured mandible.
2. Recent disruption of the hyoid bone and distortion and collapse of the larynx, probable strangulation.
3. Recent dilation and laceration of the vagina and anus-rectum, probable vaginal and anno-rectal rape.
4. Recent hemorrhages in the left shoulder and chest, partly separated costochondral junctions, probable blunt chest injury.
5. Postmortem decomposition.

The cause of death was listed as strangulation. The manner of death: homicide.

The autopsy was also performed on June 6, by Dr. McGarry on the unknown white male discovered in the water about a mile from where Nichole's body was found the same day.

This body was found to be 6'1¼" long, with gray eyes. On the left arm there was a tattoo measuring 11 × 6 centimeters of a skull and crossbones wearing a Marine cap and resting on an eight ball. Tattooed above was the name "Billy." Below was tattooed "USMC." The pathologist listed "numerous" stab wounds on the lower lip, the left side of the head above the ear, five wounds below the left ear, three wounds behind the left ear, eleven wounds along the right cheek and jaw, a wound above the right ear, a wound in front of the right ear, a wound along the left jawline, a wound in the central neck area, a deep wound on the left buttocks, seven stab wounds on the right wrist, two more near the right elbow, one in the right shoulder, another in the right hand, forty-seven more wounds along the left shoulder and arm, and the left hand had been amputated by a sharp object.

The doctor listed his provisional autopsy diagnoses:

1. Multiple recent stabbing and cutting wounds:
   a. eighty-two recent stab wounds of the face, scalp, neck, arms, forearms, right wrist, left shoulder, left inguinal region;
   b. recent amputation across the distal left forearm;
   c. recent slashing wound of the perineum.
2. Asphyxia due to drowning:
   a. fluid-filled lungs;
   b. petechiae in the petrous bones;
   c. congested cyanotic brain and viscera;
   d. dilated heart.
3. Postmortem decomposition.
4. Old tracheostomy scar.

The cause of death was listed as drowning. The manner: homicide.

As soon as the autopsies were completed, St. John detectives returned to the spot where Nichole had been found, to look for more evidence. They found nothing.

Crimestoppers, the anonymous informant reward program in New Orleans, released a press release to the local media under the caption: "Crimestoppers offers $1,000 reward for clues in Nichole Lopatta case."

Crimestoppers, which had received some success in past cases, offered $1,000 cash for information leading to the arrest and indictment of the person responsible for the death of eight-year-old Nichole Lopatta. Explaining that Nichole had been missing since Sunday, Crimestoppers reported that Nichole was last seen at a convenience store on Behrman Highway. Whoever called in did not have to give their name in order to be eligible for the reward.

At 5:50 P.M., Norman Gibbs signed a JPSO "consent to search" form, allowing detectives to search his apartment. Lieutenant Cricket Montecino, Sergeants Craig Taffaro and Sam Chirchirillo, as well as Detective Judy Long secured the following from the residence:

1. Norman Gibbs's resume.
2. Negatives.
3. Ten videotapes.
4. Two paperback books.
5. Photographs.
6. Miscellaneous papers.

At 6:20 P.M., Norman Gibbs was interviewed by Det. Rene Stallworth at the Jefferson Parish Sheriff's Office Detective Bureau in the old Gretna Courthouse Annex at 200 Huey P. Long Avenue in Gretna.

Gibbs, open and calm, answered questions without reservation during the brief interview.

"Have you ever been involved in sex with a child since you have been an adult?" Rene asked right off the bat.

"No," Gibbs answered without blinking an eye.

"Have you ever washed dishes at Nichole's house?"

"Yes. more than once."

"Have you ever gone upstairs to the children's room with the children?"

"Yes. I go up in the stupid room and try to get them to clean it up. It's always nasty and dirty."

Rene continued her questioning, pausing for emphasis when she arrived at the question: "Have you ever fondled Nichole or any of her friends?"

"No."

More routine questions were asked before another pointed question was asked by Rene: "Are you sexually attracted to children?"

"No."

"Were you sexually aroused when children sat on your lap?"

"No."

"Are you sexually involved with Jodee?"

"No, we are just friends."

"Why are you not sexually involved with Jodee?"

"Because we agreed not to get sexually involved

due to Jodee being recently separated."

"Are you sexually involved with any woman?"

"No."

Rene went on to ask when was Gibbs's last sexual involvement with a woman. He told her it was about two years ago.

"Why are you not involved sexually with anyone?"

"I just don't want to be right now."

"Have you asked Jodee to have sex with you?"

"About two weeks ago we talked about it. She didn't want to and made it clear to me that she didn't want that kind of relationship between us."

"How do you feel about this?"

"I was disappointed but I understood her reasons."

"Are you jealous about Jodee's relationship with her other male friends?"

"I was a little jealous."

After determining Gibbs drove a white Toyota Corolla, Rene asked, "Have you ever touched Nichole or her friends?"

"I have touched Nichole but if you mean sexual, I have never done that."

"Do you masturbate?"

"I don't feel that I want to answer that. I can't see why that is important to you."

After Gibbs restated his alibi, that he was home

alone on Sunday watching a basketball game, Rene asked another direct question.

"Did you see Nichole Sunday?"

"No."

"Are you homosexual or bisexual?"

"No."

"Is there anything you can tell me to help us find Nichole's murderer?"

"No."

"Are you in love with Jodee?"

"Yes, but I didn't tell her this."

After the interview, Detectives Barry Wood and Jimmy Trapani were asked to drive Gibbs back to the Tres Vidas Apartments. It was the first time Wood saw Gibbs. Unaware that Gibbs would soon become the leading suspect, Wood only knew the man as one of many questioned in the matter.

Gibbs didn't say much on the way back to his car. He politely thanked the officers when they dropped him off. Wood's impression was that Gibbs was an unassuming, not very aggressive sort of man.

Nine

Saturday, June 8, 1985.

The psychic brought to the Lopatta home by Detective Judy Long was in the limelight again in an article in *The Times-Picayune* entitled "Secretive Psychic Awoke With A Vision." Identified only as Donna, a thirty-six-year-old mother of four and Mississippi housewife, the psychic claimed to have awakened Thursday morning with a vision. Donna's vision was of the Tres Vidas Apartments, of a man in a vehicle, and of the swamp where Nichole's body was found. Donna saw Nichole's body in her vision and described it as "Morbid. I've never seen anything like that before. For someone to do what they did to that child . . ."

The paper reported on a previous case in which Donna helped New Orleans police and Picayune, Mississippi police. It also reported that Donna uses no crystal balls, nor any of the "stargazing and mystic trappings" of the stereotypical psychic.

Donna claimed to have envisioned a "wealth of information" in the Nichole case and named at least

84

two suspects. Chief Deputy Eugene Fields of JPSO already singled these suspects out. Although Donna refused to be photographed, she did consent to an interview by a reporter.

In another article entitled "Swamps searched for clues," *The Times-Picayune* updated the citizens of metropolitan New Orleans on the search of the scenes where Nichole and the unidentified white male were found, including a map of the area and a likeness of the tattoo on the unidentified white male.

The paper hinted at the FBI psychological profile of Nichole's murderer being put together at the time. Vaunted as an extremely useful tool, FBI profiles were garnering headlines across the U.S. Using statistics, the profile provides a "rough sketch" of the killer and his habits, as well as where the killer likely lives and what he might do next.

Somewhat confusing to Detective Barry Wood and others involved in the case was the newspaper's account of the profile, which pointed to an "uneducated" suspect (because the murder was so crudely carried out and because Nichole was taken so far away from home). This was confusing because Wood and other detectives had seen the preliminary profile, and it claimed the killer was highly educated. In fact, the profile seemed to fit Norman Gibbs, the leading suspect, like a glove. Gibbs had been put under close police surveillance.

Ten

FBI special agents at the Tres Vidas were still conducting interviews of children. Another girl had come forward with information about a green- or aqua-colored pickup truck, driven by an individual resembling the composite drawing released to the public. She had seen the man and truck by the Tres Vidas twice during the previous week. She described him as "creepy looking" and more "sleazy" and "leery" than the composite.

Another girl was positive she had seen Nichole at the water slide on Park Place on Sunday, June 2, around 6:00 P.M.

A total of fifty-four individuals were interviewed on Sunday "with negative results."

The St. John The Baptist Parish Coroner, Dr. S.J. St. Martin, conducted a press conference in which he concluded there was little to link the two bodies found in his parish (Nichole and the unidentified white male). "I don't think the connection is very strong," the doctor was quoted in *The Times-Picayune*. "It looks like two separate cases." He added that the unidentified male may have been dead as long as ten days before he was found, whereas Nichole died the previous Sunday or Monday at the latest.

FBI Special Agent Cliff Anderson, echoing the feelings of the field investigators like Barry Wood, stated that "The coincidence is too much to ignore." Anderson added that identifying the dead man was crucial.

Meanwhile, St. John detectives were vigorously following up leads. A number of calls had come in about men named "Billy" with similar USMC tattoos.

Psychic Donna Bray was also featured in the media blitz. Reporters could not successfully confirm that she had been brought to the crime scene to walk the area by authorities. Donna was quoted, however, saying that the bodies were related.

To the chagrin of St. John officials, the media centered on the "dumping ground," describing the site where the victims had been found as the new body dump site for the metro area.

Barry Wood and his fellow detectives, behind

closed doors, speculated that the unidentified man was either Nichole's abductor or that he may have witnessed her sexual assault or murder.

Donations began being taken by two Terrytown mothers for the Lopatta family. By Saturday afternoon $600 had been raised.

In another smaller article, *The Times-Picayune* detailed the "Naval" memorial service planned for little Nichole at the Naval Support Activity in Algiers.

In still another article, the paper reported on the "Fingerprint program kept busy after slaying." About two hundred children were fingerprinted at the Woodland Presbyterian Church, as well as many more at other sites throughout New Orleans. In response to Nichole's murder, and the media saturation of the event, metropolitan mothers brought their children forward to be printed.

A father stated, "We have been meaning to do this for a long time. But we put it off." One mother credited Nichole. "We've usually slept in," the mother said, "but that little girl helped get us up today."

Another was quoted, "We've got to do what we can to keep them safe."

Barry Wood read the article and knew, in his gut, that the only way to keep them safe was to catch the fucking killer. *Period.*

Monday, June 10, 1985.

Sgt. Robert Hay, arriving at the St. John Detective Bureau, received a report from an informant who had given reliable information to the Sheriff's Office on several occasions in the past. The report stated that the unidentified white male, found in the water near Nichole's body, was a local man named Billy Phillips, who had been missing for some time. Phillips, whose date of birth was December 14, 1959, was twenty-five. Hay quickly discovered Phillips's arrest record with St. John Parish. Phillips had been arrested for armed robbery on February 18, 1983. Hay quickly went to get Phillips's fingerprint card.

After an exhaustive search, Hay learned that St. John authorities did not retain a copy of the fingerprint card for Billy Phillips. Hay was forced to call the Louisiana State Police in order to get a copy of the fingerprints.

At the Jefferson Parish Sheriff's Office Detective Bureau, the FBI released its preliminary profile on Nichole's killer to investigators from Jefferson, St. John, and the state police. Barry Wood and Robert Hay read the report carefully. The profile described the killer as a white male, between eighteen and thirty-two years old, with a high school education, possibly some college education. The perpetrator was left-handed, holding a white-collar job, and was at least a latent homosexual.

Settled at his desk after the meeting, Wood perused the morning *Times-Picayune*, discovering an article entitled "Unidentified boy's fingerprints are taken." At least the paper was a couple steps behind them, reporting that fingerprints were taken from the body as authorities strove to identify the dead man. The paper also mentioned the potbellied forty-year-old white male in the green pickup, reportedly exposing himself to children in Terrytown.

"Jesus," Wood moaned aloud. He knew they'd been inundated again, with more reports about this mystery man in the green pickup. *That was all they needed!*

Wood was interrupted in his thoughts when he saw Jodee Lopatta being escorted into the Detective Bureau.

Jodee Lopatta was living in a fog since they came to tell her Nichole was gone. She sank deeper the more they told her about her daughter's fate. She couldn't conceive of the evil, the complete evil that had befallen her sweet girl.

Special Agents Cassandra Chandler and Gerard

Stagnato, from the New Orleans Field Office of the Bureau, arrived at the Jefferson Parish Detective Bureau to interview Jodee on Monday morning. Cloistered in the Juvenile Division Office, the agents went over Jodee's life story with her again, taking meticulous notes to compare her story with her earlier versions that she'd given to police several times already.

Her weary eyes glazed and lifeless, Jodee spoke in a quiet voice, a sad voice, giving information on Wolfgang Lopatta, Norman Gibbs, and Mark Summers. She described Wolfgang as very jealous and told how Nichole loved Wolfgang.

Jodee retold how she had gone to Po Folks with Carline Thayer, and how upon returning learned that Nichole was missing. She described Nichole as a "homebody." All of her children were described as "high strung." Jodee then listed several of Nichole's friends, all neighborhood children, advising that the Sheriff's Office had already spoken to all of them.

Jodee then advised how she and her first husband Van Orin Jarrard were divorced, how he'd slapped her once, and how she felt he would have never taken Nichole because he did not wish to even see her after she was born.

Before leaving, Jodee had something to add. She told the agents how she'd heard, a half hour before the interview started, that a man in a green or brown truck was exposing himself in her neighborhood.

While Jodee was being interviewed by the FBI, Detective Rene Stallworth was interviewing oldest daughter Jodee Bee at the Lopatta apartment, going over again, for the record this time, what she and Nichole and Samantha had done on the day Nichole disappeared.

When asked if she saw who took Nichole, Jodee Bee answered, "No."

"Did you see a man approach Nichole on Saturday," Rene asked, "and give her candy, then tell her that he was coming back on Sunday?"

"No."

"Did you see the man you gave, uh, described in the composite drawing on Saturday?"

"No."

"When did you see the man?"

"About a month ago." Jodee Bee went on to elaborate about the man in the green truck who flashed her near the east end of the apartment complex.

"Is that the same man you gave the composite drawing of?"

"No. That man had long stringy hair."

The story kept changing. Jodee Bee's eyes darted away each time she told her story. The little girl was more than frightened. She was terrified. Rene cut the interview short.

"Is there anything you can tell me that could help us find the person that took Nichole away?"

"No."

Rene was happy to stop the questioning. Jodee Bee didn't look particularly relieved. At eleven, she was faced with the nightmare that she would never see her little sister again. And it was her fault.

As soon as Special Agents Cassandra Chandler and Gerard Stagnato finished interviewing Jodee Lopatta, they proceeded across the Mississippi to interview Norman Gibbs at his Lake Avenue apartment. At that time Gibbs described his relationship with Jodee Lopatta as a "dating relationship." He then gave the same story he gave investigators on Thursday, June 6. After putting in a few hours alone in his office on Sunday morning, Gibbs returned home after 11:00 A.M. and called Jodee Lopatta. Nichole answered and said her mommy wasn't there. Gibbs did some laundry, then watched an NBA basketball game on TV. He called Jodee back around 4:00 P.M. Jodee was on the other line and said she'd call him back. She did, sometime between 6:00 and 6:30 P.M.

Gibbs described Nichole as a very "group" oriented individual and said he had absolutely no idea and could not even guess at what happened to her.

Eleven

Tuesday, June 11, 1985.

Detective Barry Wood, dressed in his typical detective getup—dress pants, a short-sleeved dress shirt, striped tie, with his new H & K semiautomatic 9-mm holstered on his hip, sat at his kitchen table and read over his morning coffee an article in *The Times-Picayune* entitled "Body found in swamp near child's is identified."

Billy Aden Phillips of Tickfaw, Louisiana, age twenty-five, was positively identified from fingerprints. Quoted in the article was St. John The Baptist Parish Sheriff Lloyd Johnson. Commenting on how the Lopatta and Phillips bodies had been found in such close proximity on the same day, Johnson concluded, "At this point I don't see any connection between the subjects."

Jesus, Wood thought. *There they go again. Politicians speaking for policemen.*

95

The newspaper also spoke of a fourteen-person task force, consisting of officers from several local jurisdictions, as well as the FBI, being formed to solve the Lopatta kidnapping and murder. FBI Special Agent Ed Pistey confirmed that the psychological profile of Lopatta's killer would be completed shortly. "We're going to have a narrow perspective in which to operate," Pistey was quoted. "We will eliminate a lot of people summarily when the profile is completed. That gives us some cause for optimism."

Wood threw the paper on the floor. *Optimism?* That was a load off his mind. He downed the last of his coffee and hurried out the door. He had an appointment downtown at the FBI office. He was the Jefferson Parish Sheriff's Office Homicide representative to the Lopatta Task Force. The veteran homicide dick was anything but optimistic.

He'd been assigned by his lieutenant. When Masson told Wood, he told him with a wily smile on his face, "Get ready to bend over. You're on the Lopatta Task Force."

Wood immediately complained, "What about Buras?"

Detective Steve Buras was supposed to be the JPSO Homicide representative to the Lopatta Task Force, but Buras had a caseload of unsolved murders, dating back to the late 1970s. So Wood got the assignment, which proved to Wood once again that the better you are, the more work they give you.

Masson, who had been on task forces before, had nothing good to say about them and had even less confidence in this one. The main problem was that everyone on the task force was so busy running around, half didn't know what the other half was doing.

The first meeting of the Lopatta Task Force was held in the Federal Building, 701 Loyola Avenue, at the FBI field office in downtown New Orleans at 9:00 A.M. Wood stepped into a conference room filled with investigators from JPSO, St. JTBPSO, LSP, and the FBI.

With the FBI serving as host, Wood knew who would be in charge. *No problem really. They had the most money.* The first function the task force decided upon was that FBI Special Agent Jim Broughton would head it. A list of participants was passed out. Wood glanced down the list, noting the names of Robert Hay and Patrick Parham from St. John The Baptist Parish; two LSP detectives; five FBI special agents; and seven JPSO detectives, including Rene Stallworth, Tony Foto, and Craig Taffaro, as well as himself. Lt. Cricket Montecino actually coordinated the JPSO representatives to the operation.

The FBI conference room became the permanent home for the task force. It was explained that members were to meet there every morning, make their reports available to FBI Special Agent Ronald Travis, and await their assignments.

Over more coffee, the task force agreed to break the investigation into four basic phases:

1. The abduction and murder of Nichole Lopatta.
2. The murder of Billy Phillips.
3. The investigation of unknown flasher at Tres Vidas.
4. The interview of suspect Gibbs.

Assignments were given out. Wood looked over the JPSO duties:

1. Crime scene reinvestigation by JPSO Crime Scene Unit supervised by Detective Barry Wood.
2. Compile list of Jodee Lopatta's friends assigned to Det. Rene Stallworth.
3. Interview and polygraph of suspect Gibbs assigned to Det. Sam Chirchirillo of JPSO.

4. Funeral services of Nichole Lopatta, scheduled for 1:30 P.M. that afternoon, would be covered by Sergeant Craig Taffaro who will compile a case file and make copies to disseminate to other agencies.
5. Compile a list of known sex offenders assigned to Det. Tony Foto.
6. Obtain a list of coworkers of Jodee Lopatta assigned to Det. Carl Armes.
7. Check Gibbs's alibi of watching a basketball game assigned to Det. Rene Stallworth.
8. Interview of Nichole's juvenile neighbors assigned to Dets. Howard Wright and John Mitchell.

Also present at the meeting was FBI Special Agent Mike Watson, who presented the task force with the preliminary profile of Nichole Lopatta's murderer. The profile came to the following conclusions:

1. The subject is a white male between the ages of twenty-five and thirty-two years old.
2. The subject lives in the neighborhood where the victim lives.
3. The subject is religious.
4. The subject is left-handed.

5. The subject is single, however, if he is married, there is an awful lot of stress in his married life. Also if the subject is married, he has no children.
6. The subject is a pedophile.
7. The subject has no sex life with people his peer age.
8. The subject is a latent homosexual.
9. The subject likes victims with no pubic hair and no breasts.
10. The subject is larger than average build.
11. The subject has an above high school education, possibly some college.
12. The subject has a white-collar job.
13. The subject is intelligent with an IQ between 120 and 130.
14. The subject, when he does have sex, prefers "doggy style" anal sex only.

Watson added some remarks to his profile. The reason Watson believed the subject was religious was in the way the killer placed Nichole's body. He wanted it to be found there. Watson also indicated that from the time Nichole was abducted until the time she was killed was between two and two and a half hours. The autopsy revealed cherry skin in Nichole's stomach.

Barry Wood looked at his notes on the profile. It read like a personal portrait of Attorney-at-law Norman Gibbs.

Actually Wood hoped Gibbs was guilty, primarily because everyone else thought so. But like a good homicide man, he kept his mind open. Evidence would solve this case, not conjecture.

During the first meeting of the Lopatta Task Force, a call came into the FBI from a woman named Parker, a black female living on Charbonnet Street, New Orleans. The woman claimed she was the lady who gave the authorities information about the Lopatta girl. She claimed she described Nichole's condition before the coroner examined her. Parker claimed to have been a psychic since she was twelve and had helped police before concerning the Kennedy Assassination, and had worked with Ronald Reagan. The woman claimed to be self-tutored and had taught at Charity Hospital's third floor.

When Wood heard about the call he laughed aloud, the third floor of Charity was the nut ward. He'd brought many a crazy person there, to get them off the street.

Before leaving the FBI office, Wood also learned of a call from a local television reporter, who claimed to have received an anonymous call from

101

an unknown female. The woman, who refused to identify herself, said that if the police wanted to catch Nichole's killer, they had to look no farther than Jodee Lopatta's boyfriend. The caller said she knew for a fact that "the boyfriend" had a history of deviant sexual behavior.

That information had an electrifying effect on the task force, like throwing gas on a fire. Gibbs was already the prime suspect.

Leaving the FBI office, Barry Wood found a parking ticket on his police car. On official business, with an emergency vehicle placard on his dashboard, along with his blue police light, he was still ticketed by the overzealous New Orleans meter maids. Employed by the Mayor's Office, instead of the police, the barracuda-like ticketers were universally loathed by nearly everyone in New Orleans.

The FBI quickly went to work on Gibbs's alibi, determining that the Los Angeles Lakers-Boston Celtics NBA Playoff game was broadcast locally from 3:40 P.M. until 6:18 P.M., Sunday, June 2.

At 1:45 P.M., Psychic Donna from Mississippi walked into the Picayune Police Department to advise the Picayune Police that a man on an FBI wanted flyer closely resembled the composite on the Lopatta case. The wanted flyer was for Steven Martin Verzi, wanted in Los Angeles for rape, burglary, and forcible oral copulation. A former bartender, laborer, musician, and telephone operator, Verzi's modus operandi was to meet a woman in a disco, determine where she lived, break into her home, and rape the woman. Verzi was last seen in California. His mug shot, which adorned his "Wanted By FBI" poster, showed a smiling man with dark hair and a beard. The Picayune Police took a report and forwarded it to the FBI in New Orleans.

On another blistering, super-humid Louisiana afternoon, Barrry Wood and Sgt. Patrick Parham of St. John Parish went back to the crime scene to search for additional evidence. Parham drove. Wood checked him out along the way, trying to determine what caliber of detective would accompany him through the crime scene. Wood immediately labeled Parham "a piece of work." Wearing thick glasses, Parham had a wide brown moustache that curled down the sides of his mouth. His brown hair was balding. Wood, who was sometimes ribbed for his slight country accent, thought Parham was a hillbilly in a state with no hills. Parham was a country boy.

On the way to the scene, Parham told Wood about a case he'd worked previously involving the death of a child. Parham suspected the mother and kept talking about the mother's reactions to his questions. Wood tuned Parham out, worrying instead about the crime scene he was about to search, a scene that had been trampled by numerous policemen already.

Wood suddenly asked Parham if they could stop and get a sifter.

"Why?"

"We're missing three teeth," Wood explained, referring to the teeth missing from Nichole's mouth. "We should sift the dirt around where she was found."

Parham stopped at a hardware store in La Place. The manager of the store assisted Wood and Parham in constructing a sifting box.

At 3:30 P.M., the detectives removed their coats, rolled up their sleeves, and walked into the woods where Nichole Lopatta's body had been found five days earlier. It was Wood's first visit to the scene. They had to work their way through the heavy underbrush.

They found the trail that led to the crime scene from a small towel left on a tree. Joined by Technician Bill Viera of the JPSO Crime Lab, the detectives were led to the scene. Wood noted that the location where Nichole's body was found was about one-hundred feet into the woods. It wasn't on the trail. It was just north of the trail. He recognized the brown discoloration on the ground where she had lain.

Although the body fluids were long gone, a faint smell of decay lingered in the humid air. Wood went down on his haunches and carefully excavated a three foot by six foot section of ground, two inches deep. The soil was sifted for additional evidence. Heavyset Viera, sweating profusely, assisted Wood. Parham helped by rinsing debris in the sifter in the nearby waterway. Parham looked like a prospector panning for gold.

After an hour of sifting, a single rooted human tooth was found. It appeared to have come from the lower mandible (jaw) and was taken into evidence to be compared with Nichole's teeth.

Wood continued his search, asking himself if this was the murder site or just the dumping site. Wondering how far clothes could be tossed, Wood threw branches in every direction, then plodded through the foliage searching for Nichole's clothes.

He kept a careful eye out for snakes and even alligators. This swampy area was infested with water moccasins, a vicious snake known to strike in complete silence, unlike its pit viper cousin the rattlesnake. The moccasin, known as the cottonmouth, grew to ten feet and specialized in striking its victim as many times as it could in rapid succession.

Alligators were fearless reptiles with a perpetual pissed-off disposition. During the crime scene search where Billy Phillips had been found, a large alligator had been spotted. The gator watched the detectives carefully, probably angered when Phillips was pulled from the murky water. Alligators like their meat tenderized, waterlogged for a while, before munching down.

Wood conducted a thorough visual search of the deep, swampy Louisiana woods. Looking for the rest of Nichole's clothes, Wood expanded his search from LA51 to the I-55 canal. He found nothing. Viera took soil samples for comparison from different areas around the body dump site. He picked up a blue terry cloth rag near LA 51. The officers remained in the woods until after 6:30 P.M.

Parham drove Wood back to the FBI Office on Loyola Avenue for Wood to get his unmarked police car. Hot and sweaty and tired, Wood found a parking ticket on his car. He pitched the ticket on the floorboard of his unit. He knew he'd get more of those, enough to make a floormat before this case was closed.

On his way home, Wood thought that whoever kidnapped Nichole and dumped her at that site had to know the area. Only the distance didn't seem to make sense. If the killer was someone from Nichole's apartment complex, or someone who knew her in Gretna, why bring her to St. John? *Unless, it was someone from St. John,* Wood speculated, *or someone who had traveled the area at least.*

Norman Gibbs entered the FBI office in New Orleans that evening for his interview. Thirty-year-old Gibbs was interviewed by Special Agent Terry Scott and JPSO Detective Sergeant Sam Chirchirillo, polygraph examiner. Chirchirillo, an old-timer, had been a detective since the late 1960s. Scott, also a polygrapher, was well liked by nearly all of the law enforcement community in and around New Orleans. Scott was extremely experienced in questioning people and had the good sense to never look down on local police, like many of his comrades.

Gibbs was asked to sign a federal form, a "Consent to Interview with Polygraph." Advised of his rights as per Miranda, Gibbs waived his right to remain silent.

Gibbs began by stating he had been admitted to the Louisiana Bar Association in 1982 after graduating from Tulane Law School. Originally from South Portland, Maine, Gibbs grew up in Kansas, Oklahoma, and California.

Gibbs met Jodee Lopatta four months earlier in an elevator at the U.S. Naval Support Facility. He had gone on base on a sight-seeing tour. He discov-

107

ered Jodee's name and where she worked on the base, called her, and went to dinner with her. Gibbs couldn't recall the name of the restaurant they dined at on the West Bank of the river, but they went to the east bank in order to dance, to the Landmark Hotel, a tall, round building with a penthouse nightclub which catered to an older crowd. The date lasted from about 7:00 P.M. until 3:00 A.M. the following morning.

Two weeks later they went on another date, to another dinner at another unremembered restaurant, this one in the New Orleans French Quarter. Jodee had met him, had dinner, and had departed alone around 1:00 A.M. There were frequent phone calls, most instituted by him to her. Once he went to Jodee's apartment to drop off flowers, but she wasn't there. He had a long conversation with Jodee's mother, Eleanor. On other occasions, Gibbs had gone out with the entire Lopatta family, including Eleanor. He had also been out with the children without either Jodee or Eleanor. On Mother's Day, he took the three girls swimming. Gibbs claimed he was close to the children, who called him Uncle Norman. Gibbs was never alone with any one of the children. On several occasions he was with Nichole and Samantha only. Although there was a lot of screaming and yelling between Jodee and her children, Gibbs thought their relationship was a loving

one. The yelling was the result of the girls not listening to their mother.

Gibbs said he spent a great deal of time around the Lopatta apartment, but never spent the night. Sometimes he would straighten out the apartment, wash dishes, help the girls clean their room.

Gibbs then ran his alibi down again to the investigators, restating everything he did that day, including watching the Lakers basketball game and calling the Lopatta apartment at 11:30 A.M. and 4:00 P.M. and 6:00 P.M., when he finally got Jodee on the phone. He was upset at that point because Jodee hadn't returned any of his previous phone calls. During their call, Gibbs heard Jodee Bee come in to tell her mother she couldn't find Nichole. Jodee got off the line, stating she had to go find Nichole. Jodee called him back around 7:00 P.M., stating she could not find Nichole. Gibbs dressed and went over to the Lopatta apartment to help in the search.

Gibbs took a polygraph test. He was asked four questions relevant to the crime, along with control questions.

The four relevant questions were:

1. Did you see Nichole the day she disappeared?

2. Did you cause Nichole's death?
3. Do you know for sure who caused Nichole's death?
4. Can you take me to where any of Nichole's missing clothes are?

The control questions used by the operators, besides asking, "Is your name Norman Gibbs?" were:

1. Have you ever engaged in any unusual sex act?
2. Before 1984, did you ever engage in any sex acts with a juvenile?

After the exam, SA Terry Scott and Det. Sam Chirchirillo discussed their findings and concluded that Gibbs showed strong signs of being untruthful on all relevant questions asked.

Near the end of the interview, Gibbs did make a confession to the investigators. He admitted he had had sex with juvenile girls in Southeast Asia during his brief tour in the U.S. Army. The juveniles were "call girls." Gibbs also stated that prior to 1984, he had "unusual" sex acts that were "kinky" but did not elaborate.

Gibbs left the FBI office, still a free man; not realizing the results of his polygraph test, along with his admissions as to having sex with juvenile girls

110

and "unusual" and "kinky" sex acts, had the same effect on the investigators as a matador waving a red cape at a bull.

Upon returning to the JPSO Detective Bureau, Barry Wood noticed several detectives passing around a photo. Scooping up the color picture, Wood saw that it appeared to be half of a prom picture. The girl in the picture was cut out. What remained was the image of a young man about twenty with brown hair parted down the center and a matching beard. The man wore a brown three-piece suit, a dress shirt with an open collar, and two-tone cowboy boots. The man had a smirk on his face.

On the back of the picture was written a name and the city of Houma, LA. Wood sat in one of the gray folding chairs in the Juvenile squad room and learned that whoever sent the photo had called JPSO the previous day.

Det. Brenda Champagne had taken the call. Wood was passed the notes of the call and wearily read them, his feet kicked up on a desk.

At 8:25 P.M., June 10, an "unknown white female" called the Detective Bureau from Houma. The woman, who had been seeing a psychic, reported that an image of a subject who had raped

111

her (the man in the photo) kept "coming up in the cards" next to a little girl with blond hair. Also coming up "in the cards" were the words "wig" and "strangled."

The caller went on to say the man had raped her when she was four and was heavily into drugs with "influential" people in Houma.

The woman gave the man's name on the phone, which Det. Champagne dutifully noted in her report, along with the claim the caller made that her phone was tapped at "about 3:38 P.M. last Saturday." She'd seen two men in her backyard near the phone box.

Although Wood's eyes burned from overwork, he continued reading, noting how the woman had also been followed by a man in a green pickup truck. The woman claimed that the man who'd raped her had raped other women and fit the Lopatta case composite released by police.

The woman added that her psychic, although unnamed, was the same one who "knew about the Atlanta murders but was never revealed." The psychic also saw "butane" in the cards and feared that the woman's house would soon blow up.

Wood put the report down and left without comment.

"Goddamn composite," he mumbled under his breath. He knew that until they caught the real

112

killer that damn composite would haunt the members of the task force forever.

One thing Wood felt confident about. *The caller had a problem, besides believing in her psychic. She actually believed that someone could be influential in Houma.*

As Wood went home, Sgt. Taffaro and other officers attended the memorial service held for Nichole Lopatta. They secured a Xerox copy of the list of 116 friends and relatives who attended the service and added the list to the growing case file.

At 10:05 P.M., Det. Sgt. Craig Taffaro and Det. Judy Long returned to the Lopatta apartment. Armed with the information that Norman Gibbs had failed the polygraph test, Judy Long had been chosen to break the news to Jodee Lopatta and interview the mother.

At the apartment, the detectives asked Jodee to step outside where she was told that Gibbs had failed his lie detector test. Jodee became emotional. It took a while for the young woman, who had just finished attending her dead daughter's memorial service, to regain her composure. Understandably, when told that the man who had spent so much time in her house over the last months was the leading suspect in her daughter's murder.

Jodee told Judy Long that she and Gibbs were never intimate and that he had never attempted anything sexual with her. Gibbs did ask her to marry him sometime before Nichole disappeared. Jodee turned him down.

"I have no feeling for him whatsoever."

Jodee said that once Gibbs had gone upstairs with her daughters to clean their room, and, once she learned of that, forbid him to do that again.

Jodee became emotional again, crying loudly.

While Judy tried to calm Jodee down, Taffaro talked to five-year-old Samantha. The youngest Lopatta girl said she did not like Norman Gibbs because he did bad things to her and made her mad. She would not give any further details, refusing to talk anymore about it. Samantha's nonspecific statements seemed to fuel the fire of Gibbs's culpability.

The detectives left after securing a promise from a still emotional Jodee Lopatta that she and her daughters would be available for more interviews when the police deemed them necessary.

Twelve

Wednesday, June 12, 1985.

At 6:40 A.M., two detectives followed Norman Gibbs and his Toyota in the rain from his house on Lake Avenue to I-10 through New Orleans, all the way to Slidell, Louisiana, a small town on the north side of Lake Pontchartrain. After taking a circular route, including a three point turn on a dead-end street, Gibbs stopped at a Tastee Donut Shop on Gause Boulevard in Slidell. Gibbs purchased a newspaper from a vendor stand and went into the shop alone, had coffee and a doughnut, and read the paper.

After, Gibbs went to a red brick office building on Carnation Drive in Slidell, went inside, and remained in there until 11:20 A.M. Departing alone, Gibbs was followed back to New Orleans. The detectives later learned that the building on Carnation housed Gibbs's attorney's office.

Gibbs was followed the entire day, leading detectives to his office, then to the Crescent City Federal Bank for a quick stop, then to a K&B Drug Store, then back to his apartment at 4:15 P.M.

A relief watch of detectives resumed the surveillance at 4:30 P.M.

The morning *Times-Picayune* reported that during the memorial service for Nichole Lopatta, friends of the Lopatta family never let Jodee Bee and little Samantha out of their sight as mourners expressed their sadness, hugging Nichole's mother and giving her support.

The thirty minute ceremony, held at the U.S. Naval Support Activity chapel in Algiers, was punctuated with religious songs and verse, including the twenty-third Psalm.

The Navy chaplain presiding over the service said that if there was any good to be found in the abduction and slaying of eight-year-old Nichole, it was an increased public awareness of the problem of missing children.

When Barry Wood read that in the paper he had one throught: *Fuck that shit!* How the fuck *anyone* could think of anything good that could come from this was beyond comprehension. *Public awareness lasts as long as the publicity lasts,* Wood thought.

116

Does a child have to die every month to keep the public and parents aware?

The twenty-third Psalm ran though Wood's mind the rest of the morning, through coffee, all the way to work. "Yea, though I walk through the valley of the shadow of death, I will fear no evil." *Yeah. Sure! Nichole never made it through the valley.* "Surely goodness and mercy shall follow me all the days of my life." *Goodness? Mercy?* "And I will dwell in the house of the Lord forever." Wood hoped so. Nichole's stay on earth had ended in the bowels of an unimaginable hell.

Nichole's body was not present at the memorial service. Her body, the remains of what once was a vibrant little girl, was too important a piece of evidence to be buried. It remained in the morgue.

Another article ran in *The Times-Picayune* that morning, "Man's ID provides no clues." Again, Sheriff Lloyd Johnson of St. John Parish restated his belief that there was no connection between the deaths of Nichole Lopatta and Billy Phillips.

At 10:00 A.M., another meeting of the Lopatta Task Force was held at the New Orleans FBI office. Attending this meeting with task force members was Dr. McGarry, the Orleans Parish Forensic Patholo-

117

gist who performed the autopsy on Nichole. He presented the results of his findings to the gathered investigators.

1. There was discoloration on the shoulder and upper chest of Nichole's body, which may have been caused by her being held down with force.
2. Nichole's jaw was fractured, caused from compression from the side by the application of great pressure causing the jaw to snap at its weakest point. There was no injury to the skin covering the point where the jaw was broken. The break in the jaw caused five teeth to be dislodged. Four were found in the larynx. The fifth tooth was found at the crime scene by Det. Barry Wood of JPSO.
3. Nichole's skull was fractured, which may have been caused by the head being slammed down on a hard surface.
4. There was bruising in the inner surface of one of Nichole's thighs, which may have been caused by the thighs being forcibly spread apart.
5. The vagina and rectum showed evidence of penetration with hemorrhaging to the extent that the doctor surmised that penetra-

tion occurred while the child was still alive.

6. There was no semen remaining in the vagina. Since maggots had invaded the area, they would have devoured such had it been there.
7. The victim's hymen was intact prior to penetration.
8. There was cherry skin in Nichole's stomach, along with food, surmising she was killed between one and a half to two hours after she ate the cherries.
9. There was an indication, from X Ray, that there might have been a prior fracture of Nichole's elbow.
10. The front of Nichole's neck showed strangulation marks, and this was caused by pressure applied to the front part of her neck.
11. The cause of death was strangulation applied from the front.
12. The manner of death was homicide.

After delivering his results, McGarry fielded questions. He quickly added that, according to the victim's mother, Nichole ate cherries at about 4:30 P.M. on June 2.

Before leaving, McGarry presented FBI SA Timo-

119

thy Herlocker with evidence he had secured at Nichole's autopsy. These "smears" were taken with cotton swabs and put in plastic tubes.

McGarry presented:

1. Oral smear.
2. Vaginal smear.
3. Rectal smear.
4. Stomach smear.
5. Vaginal removed smear.
6. Rectal removed smear.

On its second day, the task force assignments centered around Norman Gibbs. FBI Special Agent Vic Harvey was assigned to interview Gibbs that day, while other investigators checked every known associate of the quiet attorney, as well as neighbors. JPSO Detectives Tony Foto and Howard Wright were assigned to surveillance duty on Gibbs.

Other officers were assigned to follow up a host of other leads, from hitchhikers from Morgan City, Louisiana, to flashers in all parts of metropolitan New Orleans.

When Barry Wood learned of the results of Gibbs's polygraph exam from eager mouthed juvenile officers and FBI agents, he realized how bad a position Gibbs, an experienced attorney, had put himself in. He was definitely the favorite whipping boy now. Suspect Number One! Wood, who wasn't so sure about polygraphs, had seen polygraphs screw up good investigations in the past. Lazy investigators relied on the "magic bullet" of the lie detector, instead of beating the bushes for clues.

What if Gibbs was guilty of molesting the Lopatta girls, Wood thought, *and wasn't in any way involved in the murder? What if that caused him to react unfavorably to all questions?* After all, the murder of Nichole was what was important. *Who kidnapped Nichole? Who raped and murdered that trusting eight-year-old with wide innocent eyes and honey-colored hair?*

Wood feared that they just might have a suspect who molested the girls but was completely innocent of murder.

Jesus! Wood thought. *What a fucked up world.*

Barry Wood was assigned to interview Carline Thayer, the friend who had accompanied Jodee Lopatta at Po Folks on the evening of Nichole's abduction. From the beginning, Carline's statement concentrated on Norman Gibbs. Friendly enough to accompany Wood to the JPSO Detective Bureau, Carline was quick to volunteer information concerning Gibbs.

121

Formerly a roommate of Jodee Lopatta at the U.S. Naval barracks, Carline first met Gibbs either in February or March. She said she did not like him from the start. Gibbs was too nice. He acts like he listens to people, but doesn't.

"He's sleazy," Carline said. He would come over to the Lopattas, take Eleanor and the kids out to do things, and just kept hanging around. Carline suspected Eleanor of telling Gibbs about any man whom Jodee went out with.

Carline immediately thought of Gibbs as a suspect as soon as Nichole disappeared. She credited her suspicions to reading about past child abuse profiles in books. She read the material because she was a mother of three herself. Carline advised that, according to her readings, a sexually abusive person was described as being very kind, always available, too good to be true, and always doing things with the children. Gibbs was that type of person.

Last Thursday, (June 6), as Jodee was getting ready for a news interview, Carline arrived at the Lopatta house, which was full of friends. Carline found Gibbs sprawled out on Eleanor's bed, "as if he owned it." Gibbs told Carline that the police were bringing a psychic around and that he felt it was of little use. He left before the psychic arrived.

On the night they were told that Nichole was dead, Carline and friends took turns trying to calm

Jodee down. Jodee, sitting at the kitchen table, was shattered.

Eleanor, who was sitting on the sofa, had Gibbs at her feet. Sitting on the floor next to Nichole's grandmother, Gibbs kept rubbing the old woman's leg "tenderly" as if to console her.

When the police searched Gibbs's car on the night of June 7, Carline spoke to Gibbs afterward and quoted him as saying, "I made all of the mistakes that an attorney would not do!" Carline felt Gibbs was arrogant and smug about the search, repeating, "Can you believe that I am a suspect in this?" Although he protested aloud, Gibbs didn't seem particularly worried.

Gibbs used to send roses to Jodee, who would exclaim, "Can you believe this?" Carline was certain Jodee and Gibbs were never intimate. Jodee did, however, state that Gibbs proposed to her.

In a shaken voice, Carline then related the events of June 2, of going to the Lopatta's, of going with Jodee to Po Folks, and of returning to be told by Eleanor that Nichole had not come home and could not be found.

Carline credited Jodee with being a loving, outgoing mother who did not believe Norman Gibbs was involved in the abduction of Nichole. At one point, however, Jodee had said that it was possible that Gibbs "touched" her daughters. Jodee would not

123

elaborate.

Jodee Lopatta was reinterviewed that afternoon by Rene Stallworth, providing information again about her ex-husband, her estranged husband, and men she knew, as well as all of her friends and associates. Some of these same friends were being interviewed at the same time.

Back at the FBI, calls were being received concerning the man in the green pickup, which were logged and dutifully followed up.

By 2:00 P.M., St. John Detective Sergeant Patrick Parham was following up two other leads. A Metairie doctor called the task force because he overheard one of his patients discussing a person who may have been involved in the rape of a child. Afterward, he followed up another lead involving someone who saw someone else pick up a "suspicious" hitchhiker in the area where Nichole's body was discovered, on a date between Nichole's disappearance and the discovery of her body.

At 2:45 P.M., Parham, accompanied by LSP Troopers Al Martin and Steven Monachello, arrived at the Metairie doctor's office. The doctor took the officers aside and asked them to keep the interview

124

"low-key," so as not to frighten or excite the potential witness. The officers then met a middle-aged white female who immediately stated she would not identify herself.

"No," she said, "I'll do this my way." Without further prodding, the woman crossed her arms and relayed her story. At 6:00 P.M., on the evening Nichole disappeared, the woman attended mass at St. Edward The Confessor Catholic Church on Transcontinental Drive in Metairie. After parking next to an old green Dodge pickup truck, the woman went into mass, sitting two or three rows in front of a man in green work clothes.

During the mass, the woman heard a male voice speak behind her in a barely audible tone. "Justice be done," the man said.

"Or at least something like that," the woman said.

Then four times in repetition, the same male voice said, "I could not enter the child's body, because he had done it first."

When asked to repeat what the man said, the woman changed her statement, "He said, 'I could not enter the child's body until we were in the swimming pool.' "

Although the woman wasn't sure who said the words exactly, the detectives secured a quick description of the man in the green work clothes and

125

left. The man was described as white and clean shaven.

Before leaving the officers secured the license plate number of the woman's car and got her name, address, and driver's license information, dutifully entering the information with their report.

At 3:00 P.M., St. John Detective Sergeant Robert Hay and Captain Oubre headed a team of officers canvassing the spot were Nichole's body was found once again. Dr. McGarry, in his examination of Nichole's body, found hair and fibers on the cadaver.

The officers searched the area first, then excavated soil once again. JPSO Crime Lab Chief Ron Singer had six-hundred pounds of dirt excavated and brought to the Crime Lab. His entire crew went on their hands and knees with tweezers, removing anything from the dirt. They were dedicated to finding trace evidence from the dirt, no matter how miniscule.

The officers found more pornographic books in the area, on the north side of the dirt road, about three feet east of the path where the body had been found, and secured them into evidence:

1. One green paperback book entitled *Teacher's Hot Wet Panties* dated June 1985.

2. One *Companion* magazine dated July 1985.
3. Three magazine photos of nude females performing oral sex.
4. One plain brown paper bag (magazine type).

At 5:40 P.M., Det. Sgt. Parham met and interviewed the pastor of St. Edward The Confessor Church. The pastor had no firsthand knowledge of the incident in his church, but thought the woman had a very active imagination.

At 11:00 P.M., Det. Sgt. Parham finished off his day interviewing Carl Foster, a fifty-three-year-old security officer at the Mark Twain II Apartment Complex in River Ridge, just west of Metairie. Foster stated he had picked up a hitchhiker on June 5, at about 8:30 P.M. on I-55 just before its junction with I-10 in St. John The Baptist Parish. Parham secured a description of the hitchhiker, also learning that the hitchhiker had luggage.

The New Orleans FBI office received a typewritten letter earlier in the day. Dated "Monday," the letter was addressed to the Federal Bureau of Investigation, 701 Loyola Avenue, N.O., LA.

Gentlemen:
Last night I had an unusual experience in

127

regard to the murder of Nichole Lopatta.

I definitely know that I am a SENSITIVE. Whether or not I am a Psychic I do not know. I was awakened about midnight and had a vision of this murderer. He is or just past middle age and is heavyweight. He is living and hiding in a small yellow shotgun house. He has painted his face black and has a wig.

Whether or not you wish to pursue this information is for you to decide. Man is fearfully and wonderfully made. If this clue leads to the finding of the murderer I will know if through the press and may contact you at that time.

Sincerely,
A. Sensitive

Wood spoke to FBI SA Ron Travis about the note, and the host of other notes received over the last few days. Travis, assigned to log in all calls and leads, quickly became the unsung hero of the task force, at least to the men in the field. He got to screen the nut cases, one by one.

Thirteen

Thursday, June 13, 1985.

Gibbs was followed again by JPSO detectives all day. Halfway through the day, while parked in a parking lot, the detectives were approached by Gibbs who told them he was going back to his lawyer's office in Slidell, in case they lost him in traffic. Gibbs then got into his Toyota and drove directly to the red brick office building on Carnation Drive in Slidell. He remained inside from 12:04 P.M. until 4:15 P.M., when he left alone and drove back home.

Earlier at 11:00 A.M., a woman called the New Orleans FBI Office from Metairie, claiming she believed her husband "had something to do" with the death of Nichole Lopatta or the man whose body was found nearby.

The husband, a fifty-seven-year-old white man, had acted "strangely" on Sunday, June 2. He went out alone and when he came home he had a cut on his hand and had torn his pants. He was also in the pos-

129

session of a girl's blouse, green in color. The husband subsequently asked the wife to go with him to visit the scene where the bodies were found in St. John Parish. The woman refused to go. She added, after giving her name and her husband's name and a detailed description to the FBI, that her husband "always commits crimes during the month of June, during a full moon."

The man's name was added to the list of suspects. SA Ron Travis, who sat through another bogus lead with patience and professionalism, took the information and filed it in the UNSUB file, the unidentified subject file.

Flowers arrived at the Lopatta apartment for Jodee from Norman Gibbs. She waited until he called to thank him.

Then she asked, "What's going on?"

"Jodee, I went in Monday, and I took a polygraph exam like they wanted and I didn't pass."

"I know. Why?"

"I don't know why. They just now made me the number one man on the list."

Jodee had to ask, "Did you kill Nichole?"

"No. I don't know who did, and I was never there that day until you called me and asked me to come over. Well, you didn't ask me to come over but I said I would. I'm not gonna lie to you. I have never lied to you."

"I know you wouldn't hurt her on purpose. Was it

an accident?"

"I would never do anything voluntarily, involuntarily, anything to the children. I am telling you I never picked up Nichole that day. I never saw Nichole that day, never."

"This upset the kids so bad. This upset Jodee Bee and Samantha so bad. Norman, please tell me the truth."

Gibbs felt panicky. "Jodee, please don't turn on me. Please."

"I'm not," Jodee said. "I want to help you. How could anybody put us through this? Please be honest, Norman, please be honest . . . at least tell me."

"I keep telling you. I wanted you bad, but I didn't do it."

Jodee paused a moment before asking, "Are you back at your office?"

"Yeah, but I'm on my way to my attorney's office."

"You're on your way to your attorney's office?"

"Yeah, well I figured after the cops . . . They keep telling me to confess."

"But. . . . Can I ask you something?"

"Yes."

"Give me a minute." Jodee collected her emotions and her thoughts before asking, "Why wouldn't you look at Nichole's picture?"

"Jodee . . ."

"Just tell me why."

"Jodee, do you know what they were trying to show me?" Gibbs felt his voice cracking.

"No, I don't. They haven't shown me anything, what?"

"Can't you imagine what she looked like after being out there? And they were describing her condition, and flies and maggots — "

"Okay, enough." Jodee cut him off.

"I'm sorry," Gibbs apologized. "Don't go away . . . I'm sorry, Jodee. You know I couldn't look at that. I couldn't look at anybody with a picture like that. Especially not somebody I knew. You know I don't even go to horror movies. I don't like blood movies, and I'm not gonna look at something like that. What they wanted. . . . Boy, you know you were right when you said it would hurt. Boy, I never imagined it would be like this."

"Norman," Jodee's voice began to fade. "I didn't either."

"Call me back after around 1:00 P.M., okay? Is that when you're going to get back from your lawyer's office?"

"That's out in Slidell, I probably won't get back till 2:30 or 3:00 P.M. I don't know what they're waiting for, chances are they're probably gonna arrest me because it's . . ."

"Arrest you for the murder of my daughter?" Jodee's voice rose again.

"And I want you to prepare for it if you can."

"All right. But I don't understand about the polygraph test."

"I don't either. . . . The policeman came over to my

apartment, and he started telling me how you. . . . He said, 'What if I told you that she's been sleeping around with all these other men. The only one she wouldn't was you.' That's the type of tactic they use."

Gibbs stopped. So Jodee said, "I just want the truth no matter what it is. 'Cause I can't stand this carrying on anymore. Somebody murdered Nichole. Somebody murdered her brutally, brutally."

"Why would I hurt you? I couldn't, Jodee, I love you; I told you that, I would never hurt you. Never. No matter what happens, no matter what anybody says, never." Gibbs's voice, raised in emotion, abruptly stopped with, "I gotta go."

"All right."

"Love you. Bye-bye."

Later Jodee called Gibbs back to ask how it went with his lawyer.

"Well," Gibbs said, "the FBI wants to go through my car and my apartment. My attorney said to let them. I guess they want to get their lab work done."

"What did your attorney have to say?"

"He asked me if I had anything to hide and I said no, and let's go for it. But I mean, the only thing I got illegal in the place is fireworks and they already know about it. What they're looking for is blood or clothing. I don't know. After they didn't find anything the first time, I don't know why they want to look again."

"Do you know what Nichole was wearing?" Jodee asked.

"I didn't even see her."

"That's right." Jodee quickly corrected herself.

"I tried calling earlier, but you weren't in. Gee, that's a long drive out to Slidell. Followed all the way. Followed back and they're sitting out there right now. I've been under surveillance ever since I left the FBI building Monday.

"My attorney asked me if I knew that I violated every rule."

"What do you mean you violated every rule? For an attorney?"

Gibbs gave her the old law school lesson. "You never talk to them, no matter what they got. No doubt in my mind their whole investigation changed when I failed that polygraph. They're no longer trying to find who did it. They're just now trying to prove I'm guilty. And they will do everything and look up anything to prove I'm guilty. You know, they're no longer concerned with anything else. I mean the original picture or drawing of the truck—forget that, they're not investigating that."

"Well, what are they concerned with?"

"When I failed the polygraph, and I have no alibi, I am the number one suspect. And my attorney talked to the FBI Agent Harvey. As far as they're concerned, I'm guilty. That's it, end of story. They're just looking for something to wrap up the case. So the only thing that could help me is this forensic evidence. If it absolutely shows that I wasn't the one, that would be great. I mean, they asked me for hair samples. They want to take a blood test, by the way; see if I match any blood, but mine is O positive, the most common blood type. Anyway, you know at this point go, do whatever they want, but I'm never gonna be out from under the cloud anyway. And you'll always suspect me, I know so. Even if I did not do it and they're finally convinced I didn't do it, you will always suspect I'm guilty."

As the sun set, sending orange and red streaks across the south Louisiana sky, Barry Wood kept a prearranged meeting with a man he had nicknamed Spade. Entering Morning Call Coffee Stand behind Lakeside Shopping Center in Metairie, Wood fanned his jacket to capture some of the air-conditioned air.

Spade was already waiting at a table in the far corner of the small coffee shop. A former JPSO officer, Spade was a veteran homicide investigator, a rare homicide man who'd left with a perfect solution record.

Smiling at his old buddy, Spade waved Wood over and immediately ordered a steamy coffee-and-chicory *café au lait* from one of the white-clad waiters. Spade was such a regular at Morning Call, he used subtle hand signals for refills. Wood placed his portable radio on the small table and sat with his back to the wall.

"So," Spade began, putting down the sports section of *The Times-Picayune*, "What is it?"

Spade, a dark-complected New Orleans French-

135

man, often spoke in black ghetto slang from his days on the street.

"Man, you're not going to believe the fuckin' case I'm working now."

"Little girl?"

Spade might have been away from the action, but he wasn't that far away.

"Man, this one's a ball buster."

Wood's voice seemed to pick up a slight country accent when he was tired, which made him appear more like Sam Elliot than usual. Over steamy cups of coffee, Wood told Spade about Nichole Lopatta, about the disappearance, about the frantic search around the apartment, about the psychic, about the children's stories, about the man in the green truck, about the harried mother, about the lawyer who'd flunked the polygraph.

"Fuck the polygraph," Spade snarled. "Remember that case on the West Bank, the wife who'd had her husband iced?"

Wood remembered the case from his rookie year in Homicide.

"She passed two polygraphs. One under a fictitious name." Spade went on to cite four more cases screwed up by lazy-ass detectives relying on a machine to solve a murder.

"I know. I know," Wood finally got a word in. "I don't believe in them either."

Then Wood told Spade about the lawyer.

"Has no real alibi. And the FBI profile is tailor-made for him."

Spade, who had studied under the FBI's psychological profile system, said, "It's just an opinion. It ain't an exact science."

"I know." Wood nodded. "Only this lawyer's got some real troubles."

"The 'assumption' kind?"

"You got it."

It was an old joke between the two. It was the old "deductive" reasoning versus "inductive" reasoning thing. If there was one thing Spade believed in, it was inductive reasoning, when it pertained to homicide cases. Inductive reasoning involved the gathering of evidence and arriving at a solution that fits all the evidence. Deductive reasoning, the old Sherlock Holmes mainstay, involved arriving at a specific conclusion from a general assumption. The Juvenile Division and the FBI were famous for jumping to general assumptions.

Wood changed gears, admitting, "Actually the FBI's being fairly methodical on this task force."

He knew Spade was no fan of task forces—better the lone wolf investigator.

"That's one thing the FBI knows how to do," Spade said. "Be methodical." In his youth, Spade had worked for J. Edgar Hoover himself.

Spade dropped the subject, but kept looking at his friend in a strange way. After a fresh cup arrived, Spade prodded Wood.

"So, what is it?"

Wood let out a long sigh, stirring his coffee. Staring into the dark liquid, he told his buddy,"Man, you wouldn't believe the way someone massacred this little girl."

In a quieter voice Wood told of the broken jaw, the chest injury, the penetration of every orifice of the little body.

"Antemortem?" Spade asked.

"Yep."

She was still alive.

"Cause of death?"

"Strangulation."

"Fuckin' animals."

"Know what I been thinking?" Wood asked.

Spade shrugged.

"Every one of those holier-than-thou anti-death penalty people should be forced to see pictures of Nichole."

"Fuckin' A."

Fourteen

Friday, June 14, 1985.
Flag Day.

At 11:00 A.M., Barry Wood supervised the search of Norman Gibbs's white 1982 Toyota Corolla at Gibbs's apartment complex. Assisted by crime lab technicians Ron Singer, Carol Dixon, Louise Braun, Doug Deauzat, Merril Boling, and Joe Warren, Wood presented a voluntary consent to search form to Gibbs and his attorney. Also in attendance were JPSO Deputy Chief Eugene Fields, FBI Special Agents Vic Harvey and Tim Herlocker, as well as Jefferson Parish Assistant District Attorney Henry Sullivan.

Gibbs signed the consent search form, witnessed by his attorney. Immediately there was a glitch. After the search form was signed, the police decided to search the car at the JPSO motor pool instead. Gibbs consulted with his attorney and agreed, driving his car in a police caravan to their motor pool. Gibbs and his lawyer watched the technicians comb his car and

139

trunk, using a vacuum cleaner.

The following items were secured into evidence, each receiving an evidence number:

- One unknown hair taken from right front wheel well of the Toyota.
- One unknown hair removed from right rear rocker panel of the Toyota.
- One fiber removed from front rocker panel left side of the Toyota.
- One known paint sample from left rear wheel well of the Toyota.
- One unknown hair removed from right wheel panel of the Toyota.
- One vacuum debris from carpet on back of rear seats of the Toyota.
- One vacuum debris from driver's seat of the Toyota.
- One vacuum debris from rear trunk area of the Toyota.
- One vacuum debris from left rear floor of the Toyota.
- One vacuum debris from front right floor of the Toyota.
- One vacuum debris from front passenger seat of the Toyota.
- One vacuum debris from rear deck cover inside of the Toyota.
- One vacuum debris from driver's floorboard of the Toyota.

- One fiber left side of the Toyota.
- One seed from front rocker panel of the Toyota.
- One fiber from hatchback trunk of the Toyota.
- One fiber from right rear shock absorber of the Toyota.
- One fiber from hatchback cover bottom side of the Toyota.
- One sample of carpet pad of the Toyota.
- One sample of soil from right rear mud flap of the Toyota.
- One leaf from left side rocker panel of the Toyota.
- One sample of dirt from left rear wheel well of the Toyota.
- One hair or fiber from left front tire ring of the Toyota.
- One soil sample from left rear wheel well of the Toyota.
- One hair from front right rocker panel of the Toyota.
- One hair from rear right rocker panel of the Toyota.
- One brown bag containing gray warm-up shirt, two pair of jockey shorts (dirty and torn), and a twenty-five-foot nylon rope from the Toyota.
- One brown paper bag containing numerous papers from the Toyota.

- One sample of carpet from the trunk of the Toyota.
- One sample of carpet padding from the trunk of the Toyota.
- One sample of carpet of the Toyota.
- One leaf from driver's door of the Toyota.
- One rock from lower grill of the Toyota.
- One leaf from left headlight of the Toyota.
- One soil sample from left rear wheel well of the Toyota.
- One hair from driver's side console of the Toyota.
- One right rear floor mat from the Toyota.

During the search of the Toyota, Barry Wood asked Gibbs questions in the presence of his attorney. Gibbs stated that he last washed his car during the week of June 2 through June 7. He stopped at a Gulf service station car wash near the intersection of Interstate 610 and Elysian Fields Avenue in New Orleans. Gibbs last cleaned the interior of his car about a month earlier with a car-vac, which was presently at his apartment.

"Had Nichole been in your car since you cleaned the interior?" Wood asked.

"Yes. As recent as a week prior to her disappearance."

"Had Nichole ever been in the rear hatchback area of your car?"

"Not to my knowledge."

Gibbs claimed that the last time his car was worked

142

on was for a tune-up on June 1. A receipt for the work was found, verifying he paid for the work via his Mastercard.

Also during the search of the Toyota, Gibbs and his attorney were interviewed by FBI Special Agent Vic Harvey and Chief Eugene Fields of JPSO. Harvey informed Gibbs that one of the factors leading to the suspicion of his "involvement in the kidnapping/murder of Nichole Lopatta" was the fact that he allegedly had, in the week preceding the abduction, proposed marriage to the victim's mother, Jodee Lopatta. Gibbs categorically denied this.

"Anyone claiming to have personal knowledge of this is a liar," Gibbs said.

There was also some contradiction in Gibbs's claim he never left the Lopatta apartment on the night of June 2, after assisting in the search for Nichole. SA Harvey stated that they had information that Gibbs left the apartment around 2:00 A.M. and returned the following morning. Gibbs told him he'd better recheck with others who were there. He spent the entire night sitting in the living room with Mark and Jerry and other Lopatta friends who had come to help in the search.

Again, Gibbs was asked to relate his activities throughout June 2. He did so, repeating the story again about watching the basketball game. The interview was terminated soon after.

The search of the Toyota ended at 1:45 P.M. At that time Gibbs was asked to sign a consent search form for his residence. He did so without hesitation.

At 2:30 P.M., the police began their search of Norman Gibbs's apartment. Wood took careful notes as items were secured from the apartment into evidence, each receiving an evidence number:

- One yellow sponge mop head from Norman Gibbs's apartment.
- Two vacuum bags from Norman Gibbs's apartment.
- Seven hairs from Norman Gibbs's apartment.
- One fiber from Norman Gibbs's apartment.
- One dirt sample from Norman Gibbs's apartment.
- One hair sample of Norman Gibbs.
- One pair of white low cut tennis shoes from bedroom.
- One paint sample from beach chair at Norman Gibbs's apartment.
- One vacuum bag of debris from car-vac at Norman Gibbs's apartment.
- One pair of DEX brown shoes from Norman Gibbs's apartment.

During the search, the DEX brown shoes showed signs of a reaction to a bloodlike substance, when tested by crime lab personnel. The trace reaction was minute and it could not be determined if the reaction was from human or animal blood.

The police attempted to secure fingerprints from parts of the apartment, with negative results. Fingerprints were taken, however, from Norman Gibbs. Shortly after, the police left.

Gibbs consulted with his attorney. Obviously, the police had found no "smoking gun." Gibbs told his lawyer there wouldn't be.

Barry Wood hadn't known that Gibbs's apartment had been previously searched prior to his arrival on the task force, back on June 3 by juvenile detectives. Any good investigator knew that once the police had been all over an area considered part of a crime scene, like the car or apartment, the search has to be thorough then and there. Coming up with evidence on subsequent searches are usually taken to be tainted. Why didn't the police find it the first time around? Was it planted?

Wood figured that Gibbs's lawyer was shrewd enough to know this, thus he allowed Gibbs to cooperate fully. Wood just followed orders and conducted his search, despite its outcome, and let the DA worry about presenting the evidence in court.

Wood guessed that Chief Fields wanted an experienced homicide dick to take a stab at searching. He could get lucky and find something the juvenile detectives missed. No such luck.

Barry Wood finally got to read his morning paper after 10:00 P.M. that evening. He quickly found an article entitled, "Girl likely knew brutal killer well."

The Times-Picayune reported that a man who knew Nichole Lopatta well is a leading suspect in the sexual assault and murder of the eight-year-old Terrytown girl. The paper cited sources close to the investigation.

Fuckin' right they were close, Wood thought.

The next sentence in the article confirmed it. The paper reported the man took a lie detector test. The paper did not reveal the man's name, but stated the police were looking into whether an accomplice helped dispose of Nichole's body.

The paper went back over the sordid details, making sure to put in the lurid facts that little Nichole had been molested, beaten, and strangled. Then it added that the suspect is a friend of the Lopatta family.

After confirming that none of the law enforcement agencies would comment publicly on the disclosure of the suspect, the paper quoted FBI Special Agent Cliff Anderson, who claimed they were edging closer to an arrest with the aid of a psychological profile of the killer and analysis of evidence gathered at the crime scene.

Analysis of what evidence? Wood thought.

"We are optimistic of solving this case fairly promptly," Cliff Anderson said. That was a load off Wood's mind.

"We are working on good leads."

What good leads?

It was like reading a science fiction novel.

A spokesman for JPSO confirmed that soil samples

146

from the scene were being tested for traces of hair. In the next sentence authorities cited the scarcity of physical evidence as the major hitch in the investigation.

Not according to Cliff Anderson, Wood thought.

Anderson was again quoted about the vaunted psychological profile, citing several characteristics of brutal sex-oriented killings the FBI researchers have studied in the past. The characteristics were:

1. Victims of bizarre sex murders are almost always women and children, and the killers are men.

2. The more brutal the attack, the closer the relationship between the killer and victim.

3. Covering up the body and hiding it is an indication that the killer feels bad about the crime. The paper pointed out another lurid detail for the bloodthirsty public: Nichole's body had only a t-shirt pulled up over her head. The body was dumped in an uninhabited area.

4. Statistics show the majority of such killers come from broken homes and can rarely sustain lasting relationships with women. The killer probably lives alone.

5. Dumping the body in a remote area indicates familiarity with the area and possibly a killer who is an outdoors man.

Wood called Spade.

"Read the morning paper?" he asked his old friend.

"Yeah," Spade answered.

"They got a snitch right in the task force," Wood concluded.

"Sounds that way to me."

Wood went on about his suspicions. Ever since he started on this case, it was as if the newspaper was reading every report the police compiled.

"Sorta complicates things, don't it?" Spade joked.

"Man, you said a mouthful."

"Ever study the Ripper murders?" Spade asked.

Wood leaned back in his lounge chair. This was gonna be another long conversation.

"Only what you told me about them."

"Well, the fuckin' newspapers really fucked up that investigation, too, but that's not what I was thinking about. I was thinking about what one Ripperologist said about the identity of Jack the Ripper. By the way, this author was once a policeman. He said that the first thing every Ripperologist is going to ask St. Peter when they get to heaven is, 'Who was Jack the Ripper?' And when ole St. Pete tells them, they're gonna say, 'Who?'

"That's right," Spade concluded, "we have no fuckin' idea."

"I know the feeling."

Fifteen

Saturday, June 15, 1985.

In the Saturday *Times-Picayune*'s article entitled
"The impact of a child's murder," the paper's West
Bank bureau chief declared that the Lopatta case
was one of those rarities that touched almost everyone. It had called up charity, contempt, solidarity,
and a renewed concern for the safety of children.

Recalling how Jodee Lopatta learned of the murder of her daughter, how the young mother faced
the tragedy and how, on top of that, she was late
with her apartment rent, two grandmotherly strangers showed up at the Tres Vidas with a donation.
Stranger's donations had surpassed $2,500 by Saturday.

Pointing out how the cash was worthless against
the magnitude of the loss, the paper went on to
describe the loss of Nichole Lopatta as a blow in
the stomach of the people of metropolitan New Orleans. However, if the authorities break the case

149

with an arrest that stands up, the paper added, it may provide a fascinating study in the use of the most sophisticated investigative tools in use today.

Barry Wood, reading his paper, almost retched. The paper went on to chronicle the use of a psychic and the use of a psychological profile. Then the paper added that detectives on the case think they know a good deal about the killer already. They suspect Nichole knew her abductor as a friend of the family.

Jesus! Wood thought.

What made it worse, was the article's conclusion that the Lopatta case made worthless those countless admonitions about talking to strangers.

Wood threw the paper across the room.

Picking up another section of the paper, Wood relaxed by reading sports. Picking up the metro section he sat back and read another even larger article, this one entitled "Swamp gains notoriety as body dump."

Twenty-one bodies have been discovered in the stretch of land between the Jefferson Parish and St. Charles Parish line to just west of La Place, Louisiana. The paper called it a natural dumping spot for bodies: wooded, isolated places of canals and swamps where an alligator can devour a body before it's found.

In quick order the paper listed the recent finds: a Missouri man, who picked up two hitchhikers in Mississippi in September 1983, was robbed, murdered, and dumped near La Place; an unidentified body found wrapped in a carpet and burned was found along the Bonnet Carre Spillway; June 5, the bodies of Billy Phillips and Nichole Lopatta were found near La Place. The victims had one thing in common: They had been dumped there.

LSP spokesman Wallace Gettys suspected the number of bodies found does not compare to the number of bodies that might still be in the woods.

"Nice cheerful thought," Wood said aloud. He figured that if all the bodies that were in the swamp could just stand up and walk out, it would look like a casting call for the movie *Night of the Living Dead*.

"I could go out there today," St. Charles Chief Deputy Boyer was quoted, "in the middle of the day and dump twenty-five bodies without ever being seen."

Wood scanned the list in the adjacent article entitled, "21 bodies recovered in St. John, St. Charles."

Wood noted that of the twenty-one murders, twelve were unsolved.

Sunday, June 16, 1985.

Det. Carl Armes of JPSO learned from the local weather service at 1040 North Rampart Street in New Orleans that the official time of sunset on Sunday, June 2, 1985, was 7:57 P.M.

While other JPSO detectives interviewed several

151

friends of Norman Gibbs, learning nothing that would forward their case against the counselor, FBI special agents were interviewing Gibbs's friends in other states, anyone who was closely associated with their prime suspect. Five fruitless interviews brought them no closer to an indictment.

Jodee's ex-husband, Nichole's natural father, Van Orin Jarrard was interviewed by FBI special agents in Long Beach, California. Jarrard could shed no light on the kidnapping and murder of his daughter.

Meanwhile, Det. Sgt. Pat Parham of the St. John Sheriff's Office conducted a detailed investigation of a duffel bag found abandoned along I-55 in nearby Livingston Parish, Louisiana. All of the items belonged to a man named Bruce Boord, white male, date of birth August 20, 1960, with an Iowa driver's license. Besides clothing, the police uncovered photos of Boord, personal papers, and letters.

FBI Special Agent Joseph S. Hummel interviewed the man who had discovered Nichole's body. Conerly Mizell was interviewed at his home, going over his story once again for the authorities.

FBI Special Agent Ronald Travis secured the apartment application Gibbs filled out at his apartment complex, as well as school records of Nichole Lopatta.

JPSO Det. Rene Stallworth, accompanied by Det. Sgt. Sam Chirchirillo interviewed Nichole's grandmother, Eleanor Mallory, at the JPSO Detective Bureau on Huey Long Avenue. The frail old woman spent a long hour answering questions, some of the same questions she'd asked herself for over two weeks. Most of the police questions centered around Norman Gibbs.

Eleanor was adamant that she felt Norman was not involved in Nichole's murder. As for Billy Phillips, Eleanor had a theory: "The Cajuns probably got him."

That evening, Jodee Lopatta endured a tedious interview at the FBI office. Jodee's statement was later transcribed, filling up forty-eight pages of single-spaced pages. Conducting the interview was JPSO Det. Sgt. Craig Taffaro accompanied by FBI Special Agents Vic Harvey and Mike Watson.

Taffaro began the questioning with, "Jodee, what is your occupation?"

"I'm a Yeoman Third Class."

"And where are you assigned?"

Jodee described, again, her duties in the U.S. Navy. Her voice was strong and firm.

"And how long have you been employed with the Navy?"

"I have been a Naval Reservist for a year and two months, but I've actually been on active duty since the twelfth of November."

"And what is your marital status?"

"I'm married."

Vic Harvey had Jodee outline her marriages, in detail.

* * *

Vic Harvey brought the questioning to the day of Nichole's disappearance. "Okay, according to police reports dated June second at 8:24 P.M., this was according to Jefferson Parish Sheriff's Office records, you reported your daughter Nichole Lopatta missing, could you tell me every one of your moves for that day?"

"The police officer and I sat on the couch for about fifteen, twenty minutes to a half an hour."

Harvey interrupted with, "What I need, Jodee, is, I guess, from the time you got up in the morning. I'd like that point all the way up to the point where you called the Sheriff's Office at 8:24 P.M. In other words give me a description of what was the daily activity for Sunday, June 2, 1985, from the time everyone got up until the time you discovered that Nichole was missing."

"All right." Jodee went over it all again, reliving the worst day of her life over again.

"Did Jodee Bee dress Nichole that day, that Sunday?" asked Craig.

"Nichole dresses herself."

"Herself, okay, did Jodee Bee put anything like ribbons in her hair?"

"Yes."

"Can you describe those ribbons?"

"I believe she was wearing . . . it's a real dark navy blue, almost a black hair ribbon. It's not really what you would think of a ribbon, it's ah . . ."

"Is it a braid?"

"No, it's . . . , it's . . . I don't know what it's called, but it's fuzzy material, it's the fuzzy type."

"It's like yarn?"

"Yes, that's what it is, thank you."

Jodee became emotional and, after a moment, calmed somewhat.

"Gentlemen, I have done all the laundry in the house, I could tell you exactly what my daughter was wearing. She was wearing a burgundy-colored bathing suit, that had crisscrossing straps, and there was one ruffle that ran up the side like this."

"Diagonally?"

"Yes."

Jodee fought to keep herself under control.

"She was wearing a light blue soft T-shirt-type material, but it was a very, very light powder blue. It had a white collar on it, it didn't come all the way like the lapel on my uniform, but it came around, and it didn't stop short of where mine are, kind of stopped right here. I don't remember exactly so much being a V-neck, as, ah, round."

"Anything else on that shirt, that you could think of, I'm saying overshirt."

"Okay, the shirt, the color was white, and it had . . . , gentlemen, I'm not good about describing. It was a certain kind of stitch, it was, ah . . . "

"Like a rosebud or something like that?"

"There were flowers . . ."

"On the collar . . ."

155

"On the collar, but they were white. I would call it embroidery, you could call a scallop, you could call it . . . I don't know. I'd have to show you something that was similar to that, for you to decide."

"Jodee, at this point we've gone through what Nichole was wearing, she was wearing this little powder blue overshirt, a red or burgundy and white swimming suit, and some little white sandals, is that right?"

"Yes."

"Did she also have some ribbons in her hair at this time?"

"She had ribbons in her hair."

"Why don't you tell us about those?"

"They were a navy blue to a black color, and I believe the other ones were white, or pink, I don't know. Jodee had her hair done up so did Samantha."

"And this . . . Jodee put those little ribbons in her hair?"

"Yes, Jodee put them, and she had her hair in braids on either side. She looked precious."

"What time are we up to now, Craig?"

"We're up to 4:30 P.M."

"Wait a minute, there's one other thing about what Nichole was wearing, she was wearing a dark blue uniform skirt, that had pleats in the front and pleats in the back, two pleats in the front and two pleats in the back."

"Is that like a Catholic school uniform skirt?"

156

"Okay, in the pleating, yes, and the design, but the color was a dark navy blue, the color of your tie."

"So when you walked out . . ."

Jodee was crying now. "I realized that if Mama hadn't gone this wouldn't have happened."

"Okay, skipping, I'm going to make another big skip, 'cause we're trying to get you out of here. In a word, has Norman Gibbs proposed marriage to you?"

"Yes, on two occasions."

"The most recent being?"

"The Thursday night that they had the Hell and Fairwell at Algiers."

"They had the what?"

"The Hell and Fairwell at Algiers Landing, which was two weeks before Nichole disappeared."

"Like I told you, he denies this emphatically, to the point that he said, you said that he proposed marriage to you, then you're a liar. Does that make you want to change your story?"

"No."

"Did you-all discuss this proposal at any length?"

"Yeah."

"Are there witnesses to either proposal?"

"No."

"On both occasions it was just the two of you?"

"Yes, one was on the telephone."

"How did the kids refer to Norman Gibbs?"

"Mr. Gibbs, I mean, Mr. Norman."

"Does anyone in the complex or any of the children to your knowledge call him Uncle Norman?"

"Nichole or Jodee Bee had referred to him as Uncle Norman one or two times. I said he's not your uncle. I said he's not your uncle and I don't want you calling him that."

"Does Jodee Bee lie?"

"She can."

"Is she pretty good at lying when she does?"

"Jodee Bee gets confused."

"You think it's confusion rather than lying?"

"Jodee Bee is a very, very hyper young lady, and when Jodee Bee gets anxious or she gets scared she's going to try to please you by telling you what she thinks you want to hear."

"Okay, have you talked to Jodee Bee at length since this all occurred?"

"No, I've been asked not to."

"Did you talk to her during the time of disappearance?"

"Just, I wonder where your sister is."

"What did she say?"

" 'I don't know, Mama,' and I said, 'Honey, where were you last playing?', and she told me, 'Mama, we were walking back, Samantha and I and Nichole and Pepper were walking back, and we turned around and Nickie was gone."

"Do you believe that?"

"No, I don't think . . . not unless Nichole saw

something that would make her run, but, you know, I've tried to get Jodee Bee to tell me: who was first, who was the last one, who was in the middle, and she told me that Nichole was in the middle. It was like Samantha and Jodee Bee supposedly turned around and it was just Pepper, and Pepper didn't know where Nichole disappeared to."

"Jodee, what I'd like to ask you in regards to Norman Gibbs, did you ever have any sexual relations?"

"Absolutely not."

"Did he ever attempt to make any moves toward having sex with you?"

"The only time, Craig, the only thing that's ever been intimate between Mr. Gibbs and myself was that he attempted to put his arms around me and hold me, and just to kiss me on the lips, and an embrace. Okay, I don't mean sticking his tongue in my mouth anything like that, and I pushed him away. I didn't want it."

"You mention while we were off the tape that Norman had no desire for sex or something like that, can you elaborate on that?"

"He told me he wanted to make love to me, but he says—I thought that he said that he couldn't make love to me, because he had some kind of disease, and he couldn't make love and I said, 'Norman,' I said, 'We shouldn't even be talking about stuff like this.' "

"Why would he deny proposing to you, do you

have any idea?"

"I have no idea."

"When he drinks heavily, does he forget? Had he forgotten that he ever proposed to you?"

"No, 'cause we talked about it a couple of days later, and he seemed semi-embarrassed by it."

"Did he allow the children to sit on his lap, in an affectionate manner?"

"They did a lot of tickling, okay, they tickled a lot."

"He and . . ."

"Jodee Bee and Nichole. Samantha really wasn't engaged that much in it."

"If I walked up to Nichole, never having seen her before, or said, 'Nichole, come on let's go get some candy,' what would her reaction be?"

"She would tell you no, and I hope she would run."

"How about Jodee Bee?"

"Jodee Bee wouldn't go with you."

"So you feel that . . ."

"Gentlemen, after what's happened, I don't know what my kids would do now because I don't know how Nichole. . . . I've tried to scare them; I have tried to literally scare them from strangers."

"Do you associate with or know any guy that would be described as 5'8", 5'9" chubby, dark skin, curly hair with beard and moustache?"

"No."

"Absolutely no acquaintance would match this?"

"No acquaintance, no."

"Let me ask you a tacky personal question, but I need to."

"Go ahead."

"What was your financial situation at the time of Nichole's abduction?"

"Be more specific."

"I mean, how much money you got, were you able to pay your rent and then . . ."

"Yes."

"All right, Jodee Bee told us at one particular point, remember when we talked to her, myself and Detective Judy Long, we talked to her, she had no knowledge of anything. Then on Wednesday she came up with the green van with the bearded individual with a moustache and curly hair."

"I don't remember it being a green van. Wasn't it a green step side Dodge?"

"Okay, you're right, it was a green pickup truck. What are your thoughts about that composite and that truck?"

"If Jodee Bee went down there, if she saw somebody like that, she would describe it, all right. We played a little game of who she's allowed to talk to, because of the reporters, and she describes you, she describes Mr. Howard, she describes Janet, she describes Rene to a tee. I mean she's very good at it."

"Now, from your knowledge, did Jodee Bee not recant that and say that was not true?"

"Jodee Bee did not say that to me. The first thing

I heard about it not being true is when I turned on the television like a fool and that is when they said that part of the Lopatta family lied. Jodee Bee was next door and heard it and she came running over and she said, 'Mama, I didn't.' The next thing I knew I got a telephone call from Diane, and Diane told me that JoLynn's daughter had seen the same guy and Jodee was not lying."

"Do you remember when Jodee Bee told me that she had a dream? I was holding Sam Monday evening, and Jodee Bee told me she had a dream that a guy in a green truck with a knife took Nichole, and Sam was crying. Do you remember that incident?"

"I don't remember Jodee having a dream. I don't remember you and I talking about that."

"Jodee Bee told me that she had a dream about the guy with a beard and a truck, a green truck. Originally Sam told me that she had witnessed the truck, but when I asked her if she really saw the truck, she said that no, Jodee Bee had a dream about the truck, and the guy with a knife. Do you know anything about that?"

"No."

"Jodee, we all believe, and people that are more knowledgeable than we are."

"I think you're going to tell me something awful."

"We all believe unequivocally that your daughter left with someone she knew."

"I don't want to believe that."

162

Part Two

"They're killing children. So many children."

Sixteen

Monday, June 17, 1985.

At 10:40 A.M., Detective Steve Buras of JPSO Homicide was notified by his headquarters of a possible homicide in the wooded area, directly at the rear of Park Place Drive in Gretna. Buras, a heavyset detective with wispy brown hair, immediately packed his briefcase and scampered out of the Detective Bureau on Huey Long Avenue. Known for his sense of humor, gallows humor that could slice through the most stressful moment with comic relief, he fought the urge to ask headquarters if someone had found a new dumping ground, this one a little closer to home.

Passing Danny & Clyde's Convenience Store near the Tres Vidas Apartments, Buras didn't need anyone to tell him how close he was to where Nichole Lopatta had lived. Turning off Behrman Highway on Park Place Drive, Buras parked his unmarked Chevy at the end of the paved part of the road. He had to walk the rest of the way along a muddy shell road for almost a

165

quarter mile until he came to the crime scene.

Meeting uniformed JPSO Deputy Robert Hobbler, Buras learned that at 9:30 A.M. two employees of WQUE Radio Station, traveling down the shell road to their radio transformer site located in a nearby field on the opposite side of the Donner Canal, found the body of a white male. The body was lying in the middle of the road. Buras asked Hobbler to file a supplemental report with the information from the radio personnel.

Buras took a moment to observe the area. He noticed the road extended another hundred yards, crossed by another road that crossed the Donner Canal to the rear of Brechtel Park. Heavily wooded, the area was littered with trash and garbage, plastic garbage bags, bicycle parts, shells of washing machines, sofas.

"A regular fuckin' dumping ground," Buras said to himself.

He moved over to the star attraction of the dumping ground—the corpse of a white male lying in the center of the road. Buras took notes: Early twenties; brown, medium-length hair; a moustache; wearing a black T-shirt with the writing "Group Therapy Lounge"; a pair of blue jeans shorts fastened by a brown belt with a marijuana insignia metal buckle; a pair of blue jogging shoes and white socks with green stripes. The victim wore a ring on the ring finger of his right hand, a blue- and red-metal-colored ring with the bottom portion of the ring broken and miss-

166

ing.

Buras detailed the exact position of the body in his notes, noting how the head was lying in a large pool of blood that had been drying in the heat of a strong Louisiana summer day. Photos and pertinent measurements were taken by crime scene personnel. The only fixed points in which measurements could be taken to triangulate the exact location of the body were the bank of the Donner Canal and two telephone poles near the canal.

A preliminary examination of the body by Buras located an apparent contact gunshot wound to the right temple of the man's head, even with the hairline and the right eye. A great deal of blood was present in the area of the victim's nose. Buras left the rest of the examination of the body to the Coroner's Office.

He noted objects located around the body. Near the victim's crotch was an Armi Tan Foulio Guiseppe .25 caliber semiautomatic pistol, nickel-plated with white plastic grips. Buras took note of the serial number. A close examination of the weapon revealed apparent blood on it. A spent .25 caliber casing was found in the firing chamber. No clip was found in the weapon. Apparently only one round fired, its casing was jammed in the chamber of the weapon.

Also located near the victim's left shoe was a four-inch Elkhorn surgical stainless steel knife. Buras found markings in the shell surface of the roadway, possibly carved by this knife. The design was a five-pointed star surrounded by a circle. Buras moaned under his breath.

A fuckin' pentagram! Buras loosened his tie and looked up, shading his eyes from the bright sun. His fuckin' luck. An obvious suicide now had, of all things, Satanic connections.

Buras went back to examining the scene, noting the Christopher Ran blue down jacket located near the victim. The jacket was lying flat on the road. In the top vest pocket, Buras found a half-pint of Seagram Seven whiskey that was about one-eighth full, along with a pack of Kool cigarettes with one remaining in the pack. He also found a wallet in the jacket. Carefully opening the wallet, Buras found a Louisiana driver's license with a picture of the victim's face on it. Letting out a long sigh, he logged the information in his notes.

The victim's name was Kevin Grinstead, twenty-three years of age, 5'10" tall, 150 pounds, residing nearby at an apartment on Wright Avenue in Gretna. Other identification papers in the wallet, along with the wallet and driver's license, were turned over to Coroner's Office Investigator Bill Donovan, who had arrived at 11:21 A.M. Donovan advised that Doctor George Bodron hereby pronounced the victim dead at 11:22 A.M.

That was typical of the Coroner's Office. Why bother a doctor with the mundane task of examining a body? Let the coroner's investigator pronounce death. Buras, like his fellow homicide detectives, always noted in their report that the doctor was *not* at

168

the scene, that the investigator advised that the doctor pronounced death.

Buras also secured a green Bic cigarette lighter from the ground near the victim's left foot. There was blood on the lighter.

Donovan conducted a closer examination of the body, determining that the wound in the right temple was an apparent entry wound surrounded by apparent smoke burns, gunpowder burns, and stippling consistent with a contact wound. It was a classic entry wound with a star-shaped hole in the skin next to the skull where the bullet had entered, burning the skin and exploding it outward away from the skull, giving the starry impression. No exit wound was located, nor were any injuries found on the body. Before leaving with the corpse, Donovan advised that an autopsy would be performed at the Orleans Parish Coroner's Office the following morning.

Based on observations on the scene, Buras felt the victim had been sitting cross-legged in the roadway. Blood splatter was found on the victim's right hand and arm and along the front of the victim's shirt and pants as he sank to the ground. Buras also noted there was no evidence of any other criminal foul play.

Back at the Detective Bureau after noon on this sweltering day, Buras, assisted by Detective Curtis Snow, began the long process of following up on the life of Kevin Grinstead, to confirm the preliminary findings of the death: apparent suicide.

Snow, a serious-minded investigator with legendary

determination, quickly learned that Grinstead no longer lived on Whitney Avenue. He had been kicked out of his apartment the previous December for not paying his rent.

Buras located Grinstead's place of employment from the papers found on the body. Arriving at Cuco's Mexican Restaurant in Gretna at 1:00 P.M., Buras learned that Grinstead had shown up for work intoxicated on Thursday, June 6; was disciplined; and apologized. Grinstead worked Friday, June 7; was off Saturday, June 8; failed to show up for work on Sunday, June 9. Grinstead was described as "strange," but no further details were given. A girl, whom Grinstead said was his sister, visited him once at work.

Buras located an important witness at Cuco's, Grinstead's friend John Gregory. Gregory, a cook at Cuco's, had seen Grinstead the previous Monday. Grinstead was staying at his sister's former apartment at the Cedarwood Apartments on Park Place Drive. Grinstead was drinking and packing. When asked where he was going, Grinstead said he was going to hitchhike to Colorado starting Tuesday to see the Rocky Mountains.

At that time Gregory saw a .25 caliber semi-automatic pistol with white grips in Grinstead's possession.

"Why you in such a hurry to leave?" Gregory asked.

"I'm being investigated by the FBI," Grinstead said. "About the death of that little girl killed in St. John Parish."

"What?"

Grinstead was nervous. "I been involved in narcotics. One of them agents dealt with me in the past. He might recognize me, and I don't want to spend more time in jail."

Grinstead became angry. "I'll never go back to jail. I'll kill myself if the cops come after me." Grinstead pointed to the gun on the bed.

Gregory went over the information again, reiterating that Grinstead was afraid of the FBI because of his involvement in illegal narcotics, not the Lopatta murder.

After confirming Grinstead's staying at the Cedarwood Apartments, Buras searched Grinstead's room with the permission of the landlord. Buras found a spent casing in a box in the rear bedroom area and took it into evidence, along with other material.

Buras also found a white envelope sticking out of the front of a knapsack. On the outside of the envelope was written: "Please mail the rest of my possessions to my Moma. I'll never need them again. Thank you, Kevin Dwayne Grinstead." His mother's name and address were on the envelope.

Buras also found four live rounds of .25 caliber ammunition among Grinstead's effects. With the assistance of Crime Scene Technician Bill Viera, Buras secured hairs and fibers from the apartment, to be compared to the victim's.

* * *

Barry Wood spoke briefly with Spade that night. "You not gonna believe this shit."

Spade kicked his feet up on his coffee table and said, "Try me."

"We're pulling out all the stops to pin it on that lawyer I told you about."

"The quasi-boyfriend?"

"The wannabe boyfriend," Wood corrected his old friend.

"I've been thinking about that."

"Yeah?"

"I looked up my notes from that serial killer lecture by Pierce Brooks. Remember? Pierce says something about the degree of victim mutilation is related to the degree of closeness between victim and killer. If the victim is savagely mutilated, it's rare that an associate is the murderer. That's a clean indication of a serial killer."

Wood hadn't gone to that particular lecture, but heard enough about it. Pierce R. Brooks was a legend in American homicide investigation. The man handled the Onion Field case, as in Joseph Wambaugh's book, as well as hundreds of other infamous cases, including the Atlanta Child murders, the Tylenol murder case, and the Green River murders. Like Spade, Brooks also worked briefly on the Ted Bundy case.

"I think," Wood said, "the stupid lawyer might have fondled the girls or something like that, can't pass the fuckin' box, and don't know how to bone up to being

172

a molester. I don't think he's the killer though."

Wood let out a sigh, "We just might have a man here who's guilty of something . . . distasteful . . . and might be pinned with the whole nine yards."

"Dumb shit."

"I ain't the only one who thinks this way," Wood added. "Most of the guys feel that way."

"Except for the fearless leaders, right?"

"Fuckin' A."

Typical.

Spade went back to the Pierce Brooks lecture. "This reeks of serial killer. Victim stalked, captured, the killer or killers work themselves into a frenzy, the old pleasure from pain thing. You gotta be looking for someone out there punishing little girls."

"I know," Wood said. "We been talking about just that thing."

The operable word here was "punishing." Whoever they were looking for was . . . a monster!

"You won't believe what happened today." Wood went on to tell his old buddy about the body in the woods, the apparent suicide, the pentagram, the narcotics paranoia.

"You should have seen Vic Harvey," Wood explained. "He hears about the suicide and the Satan shit and throw his hands up in the air and says, 'It seems like we find a snake under every rock we turn over in this case.' Hell, we're amazed how many criminals and assholes have popped up in this area."

"It's the West Bank," Spade said.

173

"I know. Now we got a stupid kid who kills himself because the FBI's all over the place, knocking on every door in the neighborhood, and he thinks they're coming after him."

"Hope that's it."

"Me too."

Seventeen

Wednesday, June 19, 1985.

Barry Wood met Dr. Ronald F. Carr, forensic dentist, at the St. John The Baptist Parish Coroner's Office in La Place. Dr. Carr, after examining radiographs of the injuries to Nichole's mouth, found two additional fractures to the jaw at the rear of the mouth. It was apparent that the cause was from a severe blow. Carr explained that since a child's jaw is more elastic than an adult's, it took a strong blow administered to the front section of the jaw to cause such fractures.

This refuted the "squeezing wishbone"-type break theory of Nichole's injury.

Jesus, Wood thought as he left. *It got worse all the time.* Taking out the picture of Nichole that the police had released to the media during the search for Nichole, Wood looked at the fragile features of the young smiling girl's face and wondered, as all good homicide dicks have wondered, *who . . . who could have done such a thing?*

The Times-Picayune ran an article entitled "Skating to benefit Lopattas." It was a short article detailing how a local skating rink was holding its second benefit for the family of Nichole Lopatta. Spade read the article, noting the touching way it described how the skating rink would turn over its profits to the family, how its employees would donate their time and even how the manager of the Tres Vidas Apartments told Mrs. Lopatta she need not worry about falling behind in her rent payments anymore.

Like his buddy, Barry Wood, Spade felt a hollow, hungry feeling inside. *The killer was still out there! The fuckin' killer was walking around, like a damn time bomb.* Spade and Wood realized that Billy Phillips had to be connected to the Lopatta case and could have been in on the killing, but someone killed him.

"So that suicide was solid or what?" Spade asked Wood over the phone that evening.

"Yeah. He told a couple people he was on the run. The bullet matched his gun, and we found a suicide note."

"Good. You didn't need that pentagram shit all over the papers."

"Fuckin' A. We got psychics coming out of our

176

ass. Supervisors going off half-cocked solving this by guesswork, a Satanic suicide, *and* today we find out that someone's going back to the crime scene and leaving porno magazines in the woods where Nichole was found."

"What?"

Wood explained how St. John detectives, including Bob Hay, had returned to the crime scene that afternoon, responding to a report that more pornography had been found in the woods. They found a new issue of a magazine *Video-X,* with two pages torn from it, lying on the ground next to the magazine. On the two pages were photos of nude individuals performing sex acts. Beneath the magazine they found a paperback book, entitled *Turned on Mothers.* There was a drawing of two women on the cover.

"They also found porno material out there back on June 12," Wood added.

"Jesus Fuckin' Christ!"

"Exactly."

Thursday, June 20, 1985.

Detective John Mitchell of JPSO spent an unproductive day chasing a red herring lead.

A twenty-year-old white woman who lived near

177

the Tres Vidas Apartments reported that she had knowledge of a known sex offender who just may have been involved in the Lopatta murder. She knew the man only by his first name "Greg." She also knew that Greg had been recently arrested as a sexual offender and had stayed in a mental hospital.

When shown the mug book of recent white male sex offenders, the woman immediately picked out a twenty-three-year-old man as "Greg." This man had indeed been arrested in Jefferson Parish the previous November for Aggravated Rape and Crime Against Nature.

Accompanied by Det. Howard Wright, Mitchell proceeded to Meadowcrest Hospital and interviewed personnel in the Admit Records Division. Mitchell learned that Greg was admitted to the hospital on May 24 and discharged on June 3, the day after Nichole disappeared. Greg was eliminated as a suspect.

Friday, June 21, 1985.

A subsequent known sex offender was not as easily eliminated as a suspect.

Eugene Richards surfaced as a suspect for several reasons. He lived in an apartment complex near the Tres Vidas. He had a medical background and on occasion was seen portraying himself as a doctor. He also admitted knowing Nichole Lopatta.

Richards, a thirty-eight-year-old white male, stood 5'9" tall, weighed 180 pounds, and had black hair and blue eyes. Interviewed at the New Orleans FBI Office on June 20, Richards stated he was a repairman for a company out of Houston, Texas. He immediately admitted he knew Nichole Lopatta, and remembered seeing Nichole around his apartment complex.

FBI Special Agent Joseph S. Hummel immediately had Richards put his activities of June 2 on the record. Richards said he got out of bed at 10:30 A.M., had something to eat with his wife, and then went swimming with his wife in the pool at their apartment complex. At 1:00 P.M., Richards left his wife in the pool and went to a nearby grocery store to buy some drinks. He produced a receipt from an A&P Store dated June 2, 1985, 1:32 P.M. Returning home, Richards "made a couple drinks," walked the dog, and returned to the pool by 2:00 P.M. He gave the name of a neighbor who could verify he walked the dog at the time he claimed.

Richards claimed to have remained by the pool until 5:30 to 6:00 P.M., and was observed there by several resident neighbors. He went into his apartment with his wife and remained there (watching the movie *Rhinestone*) until 8:45 P.M., when he and

179

his wife went to pick up his stepdaughter and her boyfriend at their apartment off LaPalco Boulevard in Gretna. The four of them went to a Baskin & Robbins Ice Cream Parlor on Carol Sue Boulevard, arriving at about 9:30 P.M.

After dropping his wife off at home (her sunburn was bothering her), Richards drove his stepdaughter back to her apartment. Returning to his apartment complex, Richards met and spoke with JPSO Captain Roger Adams around 10:00 P.M. Capt. Adams was heading the search for Nichole Lopatta at the time. From 10:05 P.M. until after 1:00 A.M., the following morning, Richards aided in the search for Nichole.

Richards went on to detail his activities of the next day, providing proof that he had to sign for a package in Kenner, how he worked with some co-workers who could verify that, and how he had been beeped and had to deliver equipment in Chalmette, south of New Orleans around 3:00 P.M.

Richards then explained that he was in the "witness protection program" in 1982-83. He entered the program in Texas and was relocated to New Mexico under a fictitious name. He gave the name of the FBI special agent who handled him later in Louisiana.

A check of Richards's story failed to indicate that any person with his name or the fictitious names

180

Richards provided was ever in the FBI's witness protection program. Richards stuck to his story. When asked what was the reason he was in the witness protection program, Richards refused to answer.

He did, however, admit to being arrested for driving while intoxicated and second degree assault on a fifteen-year-old. He added that the assault charge had been dropped.

FBI Special Agent Dallas Kunkle conducted an immediate investigation of Richards, learning that Richards was wanted by Michigan authorities on a nonsupport warrant from May 1984. A deputy with the Iosco County Sheriff's Office in Tawas City, Michigan, who claimed to be familiar with Richards, stated Richards had been involved in criminal sexual conduct involving a younger female.

The deputy added another piece to the puzzle. In 1979 or 1980, while on patrol, the deputy spotted Richards in a rural cemetery with a seventeen-year-old girl. When stopped and questioned, the girl said that Richards was a doctor and was going to give her a physical examination in the cemetery.

Richards apparently worked in medical service for retired individuals while up North. The deputy believed Richards had the psychological makeup to commit a violent act.

While the FBI was concentrating on this new suspect, JPSO's Rene Stallworth was conducting deep background investigative work on some of the girls who were friends of Nichole Lopatta, trying desperately to uncover any information in the lives of the little girls that would surface the killer.

A large picture in the morning *Times-Picayune* showed children skating in a roller rink. It was the fund-raiser for Nichole Lopatta's family.

Eighteen

Saturday, June 22, 1985.

The Times-Picayune ran an article entitled "Arrest in girl's slaying still on hold." The article began with a statement that sounded like a complaint. An arrest in the death of Nichole Lopatta seemed imminent a week ago, yet no one has been charged with her abduction, sexual assault, and strangulation.

Declaring that information has been hard to obtain from closemouthed investigators of the Lopatta Task Force, the paper went on to state that sources close to the investigation still insist their leads are encouraging, and the chance of arrest and conviction were good.

Barry Wood put his morning coffee down and had to keep himself from laughing aloud. *The paper was un-be-fuckin'-lievable! Close to arrest AND conviction? Un-fuckin'-real!*

He read on anyway. The paper was more entertaining than the science fiction novel he'd been reading lately. The novel took place on a desert planet named Arrakis. *Hell,* Wood thought, Dune *was infinitely more realistic than the paper.*

According to the paper, the big problem facing the task force was the lack of physical evidence. *No fuckin' kidding!* There was a leading suspect, a man who knew Nichole and her family. The paper quoted sources that the man failed a polygraph test.

Wood wasn't laughing anymore. If there was any doubt that the paper had an inside source, it was erased that morning.

FBI Special Agent Cliff Anderson was quoted as saying that they believed Nichole was lured away from her home by a promise of reward. But a failed lie detector test, an accusation by a Mississippi psychic, and an FBI psychological profile that fit the suspect were not enough to jail a man, according to the paper.

Well, they knew something Wood didn't. He didn't know for sure that the psychic had named Norman Gibbs. Apparently she had.

Wood's boss was quoted next. JPSO Chief of Detectives Eugene Fields claimed there were no snags. "We're waiting on our evidence." The paper went on to explain about how the FBI was analyzing soil from the crime scene.

Then the paper put in the kicker. Something known

184

to only a very few. On June 14, clerks of the Orleans Parish Coroner's Office released the body of Nichole Lopatta to a local funeral parlor. The House of Bultman Funeral Home removed the body and cremated the remains of Nichole Lopatta. Jodee Lopatta was shocked, more than shocked. So were most of the investigators.

A valuable piece of evidence was now gone. Wood, like any good homicide dick, understood that the body of a murdered victim was just that — a valuable piece of evidence.

What the paper didn't say was that no one knew who authorized the release of the body. There had been a call to the Coroner's Office and a call to Bultman's. There had to have been a call, everyone agreed. Only no one remembered receiving a call, and no one knew if the caller was a man or a woman.

Jodee Lopatta went ballistic. She demanded to know what happened, who ordered it and why. Jodee wanted to say her last goodbyes to her Nichole before cremation. This devastated the already distraught young mother.

Monday, June 24, 1985.

The FBI continued their investigation of Eugene Richards, learning he had worked for a medical service company in Michigan. Richards had been fired in 1981 for not showing up for work. An employee in the personnel division elaborated that Richards did not show up for work because he was in jail on a sexual matter involving a young female. The personnel employee went on to explain that he indeed remembered Richards, describing Richards as a man who presented himself as a clean-cut type, a very competent individual. Only, once one became familiar with Richards, one learned he was a pathological liar.

Authorities in Michigan confirmed that there was a warrant for the arrest of Eugene Richards for Assault With Intent to Commit Criminal Sexual Conduct. The matter had not been pursued after Richards moved out of the area. Further investigation revealed the details of the accusation against Richards.

Back in September 1981, thirty-five-year-old Richards was accused of forcing a fifteen-year-old girl to have sexual relations with him. Additionally, Richards had used a seventeen-year-old male to initiate contact with the victim. The crime allegedly occurred in Richard's van. After the crime, the girl went home and called police. Richards was apprehended after he tried to get away on foot. When apprehended near his vehicle, the police discovered a jungle knife, a first aid kit, a fillet knife, sleeping bags, and miscellaneous medical supplies.

Richards denied the accusation.

Barry Wood's assignment that Monday was to ascertain the whereabouts of a known sex offender, a man who had been arrested in Jefferson Parish for kidnapping, aggravated rape, and aggravated crime against nature. It took Wood several hours to verify the fact that the man had been sentenced to fifteen years hard labor without benefit of probation, parole, or suspension of sentence in April 1980.

Several phone calls to Angola State Penitentiary confirmed the man was still in custody.

Another day. Another dead-end lead.

Tuesday, June 25, 1985.

The following day, Wood went about verifying if the receipts that Norman Gibbs had in his vehicle were authentic. Wood went to Trahan's Texaco Station and spoke to several employees about the mechanical work on Gibbs's Toyota.

No one could recognize Gibbs from the Polaroid Wood carried with him. The register receipts could not be authenticated, since they were forwarded to Texaco. The mechanic on duty at the time Gibbs's car had been worked on did not recognize Gibbs nor remembered the Toyota, but said he could have worked on a Toyota that day.

Another useful day, Wood felt, returning home that evening.

He reminded himself that the paper felt they were close to an arrest. *The suckers.*

Earlier that day, while Wood was running down gas station receipts, FBI special agents were reinterviewing Jodee Bee, in case Nichole's sister had anything new to tell them. She hadn't.

Still earlier, Norman Gibbs arrived at the New Orleans FBI Office. At the request of Special Agent Vic Harvey, Gibbs allowed himself to be fingerprinted. Gibbs also pulled several hairs from his head and gave them to another FBI agent. The hairs were then sealed in an envelope for transportation to the FBI Laboratory in Washington, D.C., which had become the depository of most of the evidence in the Lopatta case.

This turn in the case upset Ron Singer, the chief of the JPSO Crime Lab, a well respected, top-notch lab. Singer felt his command was being treated like stepchildren. It was they who sifted through six-hundred pounds of excavated dirt for fibers and hair. It took days, and their work was now turned over to the FBI. Wood, who sympathized with Singer, was powerless. The FBI ran the task force. *Period.*

* * *

188

Nichole Lopatta.

The Tres Vidas apartment complex,

where Nichole was kidnapped.

Composite of suspect that was
distributed by police.

John Francis Wille.

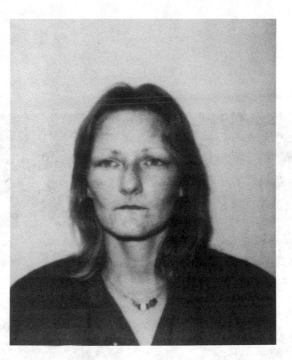

Judith Walters.

Billy Phillips.

Judith Walters's car, in which Nichole was kidnapped and raped.

An aerial view of the crime scene, the wooded area between Interstate 10, the elevated highway, and U.S. 51.

The trail on the right is the one Conerly Mizell was walking when he discovered the body.

The trail down which Nichole's body was found.

The body of Nichole Lopatta.

St. John parish detectives at the crime scene.

The Popeye's outlet where Wille disposed of grisly evidence.

Thursday, June 27, 1985.

A bizarre scene was played out at the Jefferson Parish Correctional Center at 3:05 P.M. Within the gray walls of the new correctional center (a new term for parish prison), a physical lineup was conducted. Standing among the six men in the lineup was Norman Gibbs. The other five men were two JPSO detectives and three FBI special agents. Supervising was JPSO Chief of Detectives Eugene Fields. Other FBI special agents and other members of the task force were also present.

The featured players in the scene were three neighbors and friends of Nichole Lopatta; little girls aged six, four, and four-and-a-half. The girls, tiny in a roomful of men, spoke in faint voices as each watched the six men in the lineup.

Chief Fields asked the four-year-old, "Do you see the man that took Nichole?"

"I don't know any of them are the man because none of them have a beard or a moustache. The man that took Nichole had a beard and moustache."

"Do you see anyone that looks familiar?"

"No. None of them have beards or moustaches."

"Did the man that you saw with Nichole have a beard and a moustache?"

"Yes."

The interview was concluded after that.

189

Earlier, Norman Gibbs had agreed to be interviewed at the JPSO Detective's Office, where he provided a handwriting sample in writing down his exact movements on June 2. Asked formally if he had seen Nichole Lopatta on June 2, he said no. Asked outright if he had, in fact, caused the death of Nichole Lopatta, he answered no.

That evening, Barry Wood studied in detail the official preliminary profile prepared by the FBI regarding the possible offender in the Nichole Lopatta murder case. The profile was prepared by FBI SSA John Douglas at the FBI Academy in Quantico, Virginia. Douglas, program manager of the Criminal Profiling and Consultation Program of the FBI's vaunted Behavioral Science Unit (BSU) at the FBI Academy, was well-known by homicide detectives as a leading expert in the field.

Douglas reviewed the case material, as well as the preliminary profiles prepared by Criminal Profile Coordinator SA James M. Watson in New Orleans. Douglas's report was compiled to enhance and refine the earlier profiles.

Wood took out a notepad to jot important points.

Under the title "Victimology," the report noted that Nichole Lopatta had been categorized by SSA Douglas as a high-risk victim. This was based on her youthfulness (young age and physical size); the transient neighborhood in which she lived; lack of close monitoring of Nichole's daily activities by an adult; and information that she was previously sexually traumatized by a family member.

Wood noted the word "traumatized," wondering exactly what that meant.

SSA Douglas's next comment perked Wood's interest even more. Douglas surmised that young victims who have been sexually assaulted by adult males may openly speak of these past sexual relationships as a means of coping with their mental anguish. SSA Douglas believed that Nichole, in all probability, spoke of these relationships with her eventual murderer.

That was some conclusion, Wood thought. *Nichole spoke of past sexual relationships with her eventual murderer. What was that supposed to mean? How in the hell could anyone come up with a conclusion like that?*

Under the next title "Crime Scene Analysis," the report noted how Nichole was abducted from her racially mixed neighborhood, without anyone noticing anything out of the ordinary. When her body was found, it appeared that Nichole was placed (the word placed was underlined), not dumped, and the killer made no attempt to conceal the victim by covering her body with brush.

The "Analysis" came next. According to SSA Douglas, the place of abduction as well as the disposal site were areas that were very familiar to the killer. He had been to each of those areas in the past. The abduction site is an area where anyone seeing him with the victim would not become suspicious.

"Crime Analysis" came next. In all probability, SSA Douglas surmised, the killer did not intend to kill the victim.

Jesus! Wood let out another long sigh. *The killer massacred her!*

SSA Douglas believed the killer was primarily motivated by sexual urges. Wood figured that was likely. Douglas went on to state that the killer utilized a ruse or con to trick the victim into believing she was getting something of tangible value. However, within a short time, Nichole must have realized that the man, who she thought she liked and trusted, made sexual advances to her. Nichole rejected these advances, causing the killer to grab, squeeze, pull and push her into submission. She was in all probability sexually assaulted in his vehicle.

Fucker beat her and strangled her to death! Wood was certain of that. He'd seen the body, smelled it, examined it.

The report went on to state that during the sexual assault, Nichole in all probability felt pain and began to scream and cry out for help. This caused the subject to strike her about her head and face in addition to pushing her face with his hand, cracking her jaw.

What had the forensic dentist told Wood? A severe blow broke Nichole's jaw, severe enough to shatter a child's elastic jaw!

The killer subsequently placed Nichole at the disposal site, which could have very well been the site of the assault. By not concealing her, the killer realized she would eventually be found.

The next part was the "Offender Profile." Wood studied this part closely.

SSA Douglas began with a conclusion, the killer knew Nichole as well as her mother. Douglas noted that almost without exception, there was always something not quite right in cases of this type. Generally, there is one or more absent parent and/or some internal family problem such as financial indebtedness, unemployment, alcoholism and/or family illness. In the Lopatta case, SSA Douglas stated, the solution of the case rests with the mother. The victim's father was absent at the time. Although Douglas admits he did not have the benefit of knowing what Jodee Lopatta has already told investigators about her "social" friends, the probable killer will, in all probability, fall into her social, economic, educational, and age group.

The killer, at the time of the offense, would in all probability have been under severe mental strain or

193

stress. Stress could have been caused by failing heterosexual relationships, financial indebtedness, passed over for promotion, up for transfer, or recently transferred.

The criminal act alone does not make him a pedophile. He may have normal heterosexual relationships; however, when under severe mental anguish, he regresses in behavior and seeks out young children companions. Children can bolster his ego and change his feeling of inadequacy into a feeling of worth. However, he will later experience further depression.

Next came the "Post Offensive Behavior." Immediately after the crime, the killer had to return home and change his clothing, in an effort to destroy possible incriminating evidence. He may even wash his car. He would then leave home to establish alibis. He may have even attempted to contact the victim's mother by phone.

Wood noted how the profile fit Norman Gibbs so closely; it was as if it was mapped out for him.

SSA Douglas stated that the killer would be overly cooperative with the mother and investigators. However, once looked at as a suspect, he would cease to be cooperative.

Gibbs had been tiring of the hunt. That was apparent to all.

Emotionally, the killer would be tense, rigid, and preoccupied with the investigators. He would assist in searches. He may even become religious, in order to cope with his crime. This would be a facade.

He will find a legitimate way to leave the area, but not right away. That would be too suspicious. He will date women in order to show investigators he is only interested in adult women.

There was no overall conclusion to SSA Douglas's report. It was, after all, only preliminary. Wood attempted to count the number of "in all probability." He lost count. What he just read was a fuckin' guess. Nothing more.

Wood certainly wasn't the only one who didn't believe that Nichole's killer knew the victim and her mother well. Rene Stallworth told Wood as much.

Talking to Spade later on the phone, Wood found himself saying, "I don't know what's more unbelievable, reading the newspaper or the FBI profiles."

"The Bureau's jumping to fuckin' conclusions, huh?"

"Exactly."

Spade fed Wood one of the oldest homicide clichés, "You got to go with the facts."

"There aren't many. That's why we ain't even close."

"Remember that line in *Butch Cassidy and the Sundance Kid?* How old Butch kept saying, 'I got vision and the rest of the world wears bifocals.' "

Wood remembered the line. "But all the homicide guys, JP and St. John, don't think Gibbs is our man."

"Only the big shots, huh?"

"They might just be going through the motions," Wood said.

"They don't have any fuckin' idea."

Then Wood told about the lineup, about the quiet four-year-old girl and the loaded questions, like, "Do you see anyone that looks familiar?" Wood half expected the girl to say yes. Gibbs had been to the Lopatta apartment enough to be recognized around the complex. But the girl only talked about the beard and moustache.

After the lineup, the little girl had added a revelation to a stunned group of detectives when she said that one of the men in the lineup had been Nichole's daddy. And she was scared of daddy. She was confused. She said something about taking clothes off, but said little more.

"You know," Wood said, "a bunch of us think that Jodee Bee made that up about the bearded man in the green pickup."

That sounded logical to Spade. Little Jodee Bee felt responsible. Now her sister was gone. There had to be a villain.

Wood and Spade knew there was a villain. And he was still out there.

* * *

Friday, June 28, 1985.

Jodee Lopatta received a letter from Norman Gibbs that morning. In the one-page handwritten letter, Gibbs said he would have liked to have called, but he thought he should stay off the phone until the FBI cleared him as a suspect, which he believed would happen sooner or later.

Gibbs reiterated that he could have never hurt Nichole in any way or taken indecent liberties with any child. Gibbs referred to Jodee as the strongest woman he'd ever known. She would pull through this.

He was worried, however, about what Jodee Bee and Samantha had been told about him. If possible, he wanted Jodee to tell them hello for him. He also wanted Jodee to tell her mother hello, although he heard Eleanor didn't much care for him anymore.

Near the end of the letter, Gibbs hoped he would be able to talk to Jodee face-to-face soon, or on the phone. "I will be cleared," he assured her. He had faith in that.

"Take care," he ended his letter, "all of you."

He signed the letter below the word "Love."

* * *

Wednesday, July 3, 1985.

The task force continued its plodding ways, following up bogus lead after bogus lead, still centering their investigation on Norman Gibbs.

Jodee Lopatta briefly met with FBI Special Agents Vic Harvey and Joseph Hummel, at the U.S. Navy Station on Dauphine Street in New Orleans. She reported that on the previous day, she had received an obscene phone call from an unknown individual. Upon hearing the obscene remarks, Jodee called the caller a filthy bastard and hung up.

Jodee also provided to the agents her new address and phone number. The Lopattas had moved from the Tres Vidas to the semirural suburb of Violet, in St. Bernard Parish, south of New Orleans.

Barry Wood received a copy of an FBI lab report on the chemical analysis, microscopic analysis, mineralogy, instrumental analyses and fingerprint analysis of material secured in the Lopatta case. Evidence from the crime scene, evidence secured at the autopsy, and evidence secured at the searches of Norman Gibbs's car and apartment were analyzed.

The results of the examination were listed in seven short paragraphs. The lab found blood, in small quantities, too small for any further analyses, on a paper bag found at the crime scene. Not surprisingly,

198

the lab found no semen on the materials secured, including the swabs of the victim's body taken during the autopsy.

From a piece of cardboard found at the crime scene, the lab found two white paint particles that could be multilayered. The specific origin of the paint could not be determined immediately, but it appeared to be house paint.

The paint secured from the wheel well of Norman Gibbs's car was different from the white paint found on the cardboard, so was the paint from the beach chair at Gibbs's apartment.

The soil, serological, fingerprint, and microscopic examinations were continuing and would be sent under separate cover.

Well, Wood thought, *so much for that.* The report succeeded in doing one thing. It did not link Gibbs to the murder. There was no "smoking gun."

Nineteen

Monday, July 8, 1985.

An anonymous tip to the New Orleans FBI office surfaced yet another name as a suspect. According to the source of information, word on the streets of New Orleans was that a man by the name of Gary (last name unknown) may have been involved in the abduction and murder of Nichole Lopatta. According to the source, Gary was believed to have killed individuals in the past and was considered insane by those who know him. The source added that the victim's mother, Jodee Lopatta, knew Gary personally. Gary might live in an apartment complex and work in a warehouse in nearby Merrero, Louisiana. The warehouse was supposed to be connected to the paper cutting business.

Gary may have worked at a radio station in Florida. Reportedly a biker type, Gary hung out at a park on Coliseum Street in New Orleans.

Gary was described as a dark-complected Hispanic male, twenty-six to thirty-four years old, 5'6" tall, with curly, dark brown hair and a moustache. Gary had rotten teeth and eyes that appear to be slanted.

Reviewing the report at the task force office, Wood noted the last sentence of the description. This Gary would stick out, even at the Tres Vidas, as easily as a pink Edsel at a Toyota convention. Wood was at least familiar with the "park on Coliseum Street." In his rookie year in homicide, back in 1981, he had worked months with his first homicide partner on a case in the bowels of New Orleans's Sixth Police District, nicknamed "The Bloody Sixth" because of its violent reputation. There were four large housing projects in the Sixth: the Magnolia, the Melpomene, the St. Thomas, and the Calliope, where more than fifty thousand dirt-poor people lived jammed up against the Garden District and the mansions of St. Charles Avenue.

Wood had walked across dirty Coliseum Square, along the skid-row Camp Street section of the Crescent City, night after night with his old partner, investigating the double murder of two black prostitutes. The women had been taken from the Sixth District to the river *batture* in suburban, where they were executed. The *batture*, a colloquial term, was the old French name for the land between the levee and the river's edge.

It took thirteen months to solve that particular case, thirteen months to discover the identity of the balding man who had marched into George's Love-In Bar on Prytania Street, confronted one of the black whores, and ordered her to leave with him. The woman's friend insisted on going along. They were both found the next morning, a .22 bullet in each skull.

Yes, Wood remembered the *batture* murders well, and the long hot nights spent bar hopping from dive to dive. *Jesus*, he thought to himself. *Coliseum Square always smelled like shit . . . human shit.*

He was glad the "Gary" lead was passed to another investigator.

The FBI located the ex-wife of Eugene Richards in Michigan. The story she told was this: she had known Richards since 1964. They were married in 1967, and divorced in 1983. She described Richards as a very violent man, hung up on weapons with fantasies of violence. During their marriage, Richards often forced sex on her. On two occasions he wanted her to have sex with him while someone else was watching. On one of the occasions, Richards came home with a friend. Both men had been drinking heavily. Richards tried to have sex with her and she resisted, so he threatened to kill her. She fled to a neighbor's for safety.

202

She described Richards as a Vietnam veteran, a corpsman in the U.S. Marines. He also told her he was a Green Beret, which she knew was improbable for a Marine. Richards liked to talk and act like a doctor, and claimed to be an undercover agent for the FBI and the CIA.

Although the woman knew of Richards's arrest for sexual assault of a fifteen-year-old girl, she had no firsthand knowledge of Richards having sex with juveniles.

FBI SA Vic Harvey just shook his head and told Wood that another snake had just crawled out from under another rock.

Tuesday, July 9, 1985.

At the task force, while going through the dailies, Barry Wood spotted a police teletype. It was a national broadcast from the Dallas Police Department, Dallas, Texas, to all law enforcement agencies.

Back on June 23, at about 6:30 A.M., a fourteen-year-old white female was abducted from a doughnut shop in Dallas. The girl was working alone. There were no signs of a struggle. The cash register had not been tampered with. Her purse was found in the store. On June 26, the girl's body was discovered in a field in Plano. Nude, a preliminary examination of

203

the body failed to determine if she had been sexually assaulted. The teletype ended with a request that any jurisdiction having similar offenses should contact the Dallas Police.

Wood checked but the lead had already been given to another task force investigator. Curious, Wood wondered why in the hell didn't the Dallas Police furnish the damn cause of death! Was the girl strangled, like Nichole, or stabbed, or shot?

Teletypes of that nature were sent to the task force on a daily basis. Wood was surprised at the number of children being killed, almost daily, in America. *What the hell's going on?* he asked himself. *They're killing children. Children! So many children.*

Wednesday, July 10, 1985.

Special Agent Vic Harvey received the rental records for the Tres Vidas Apartment Complex. A list of seventy-three people was given to the FBI by the apartment's managers. The list included every renter, listing as much information as could be obtained: their name, race, sex, date of birth, driver's license number, social security number, place of employment, vehicle information, as well as who resided with them.

The names on the list were divided among task

force members for investigating. With Gibbs's arrest seeming unlikely, everyone wanted to know if they'd missed something. A serious amount of backtracking began.

Friday, July 19, 1985.

From Thursday, July 11, through Friday, July 19, the Lopatta Task Force continued its investigation of Norman Gibbs, primarily speculating on if they had enough to indict or not. The consensus was they did not have enough.

During the same period the task force continued checking out leads, following up on all males with arrests who lived anywhere near the Tres Vidas, as well as all males arrested anywhere near the vicinity, particularly for sexually related crimes.

One individual, with nine arrests, was checked out. A confederate, with sixteen arrests dating from 1969 through 1980, was also checked out. A third man, with twenty-one arrests, was also located and investigated. None of the men could be connected to the case.

Thursday, July 25, 1985.

In pursuing a lead that placed an ice cream man in

the vicinity of the Tres Vidas on June 2, selling ice cream to a little girl who fit Nichole's description, the FBI interviewed the last of the seventeen male ice cream delivery men who worked for Circus Delight Ice Cream Company. The anonymous lead, which resulted in this rousting of ice cream men, stated that one of them liked to lure little girls into his truck by offering free ice cream.

The task force concluded, after logging a "shit-load" of man-hours, that the lead was, as one member put it, "shit on a stick."

Tuesday, July 30, 1985.

Several weeks after the last article appeared in the local paper, the Nichole Lopatta case was back in the newspaper. *The Times-Picayune* ran an article entitled, "Nichole's slaying: Cops can't link suspect."

Wood read the article carefully. It started, as so many had, with a retelling of the kidnapping, rape, strangulation; of the desperate search for Nichole; and how, from the beginning, the authorities believed they had their man. Eight weeks later, they still believed it.

Some did, Wood thought, *then again, some didn't.* He certainly didn't, and neither did the homicide

206

men, the *real* homicide men. After sifting through all of the material assembled pertaining to Norman Gibbs, Wood and his partners agreed that it didn't add up to much. Certainly not enough for an arrest.

The paper went on to say that authorities believed the killer did not plan the killing very well, and was not particularly careful in covering his tracks.

Sexual serial killers sometimes do not plan killings at all, Wood thought. *Whoever killed Nichole didn't try to cover his tracks at all.* But they still had no idea who he was. Wood felt sure of that.

The paper then quoted Wood's Chief of Detectives, Eugene Fields, who claimed that they had a "top suspect," but not enough evidence to make an arrest. Detectives were working on the assumption that Nichole was killed near her house and dumped in St. John.

"If you want to cover up a murder," an unidentified investigator was quoted as saying, "you do exactly what he did—drag the body through a bunch of parishes."

After describing the body in detail, the paper went back to the suspect. The quoted sources close to the investigation said the lead suspect had participated in the search for Nichole in the days after her disappearance. He had been questioned extensively and failed a lie detector test. He also fit a psychological profile of Nichole's killer prepared by FBI sex crime experts.

Pornographic materials found where Nichole's body was found are similar to those confiscated in a search of the suspect's home.

Wood stopped a second. He conducted the search of Gibbs's apartment. Whatever porno material was taken had been taken by the FBI, not by him. He made a note to check on that fact.

The paper went on to explain that authorities believe they could link their suspect to sexual offenses against Nichole before she was abducted.

Jesus! Wood was certain of something, whoever was feeding this shit to the paper was stretching it. They couldn't link shit. Wood and some of the others *suspected* Gibbs may have molested Nichole. But it was sheer speculation.

Wood read on. The paper went on to elaborate on the Jodee Bee lead of the dark-haired man with the beard in the green pickup that several of Nichole's playmates said had molested them and Nichole in the past. This was science fiction, pure and simple. *No,* Wood corrected himself, *it was the fearful delusion of frightened children, contaminated by gossip and newspaper accounts.*

One thing made Wood feel relieved and a little unfulfilled at the same time. The paper announced that the Nichole Lopatta Task Force had been disbanded. Investigators from St. John, Jefferson, the FBI, and the Louisiana State Police would continue coordinating evidence. *But now,* Wood thought, *only homicide men would be involved.*

He reached over and picked up the three-inch by five-inch color photo of Nichole Lopatta he'd been carrying with him since he was first assigned to the case. He stared at the face in the photo: the delicate, soft face; the honey-colored straight hair; the little wide nose; the slight smile that revealed front teeth naturally separated. In the photo, Nichole wore a striped shirt.

Wood felt his stomach twist. He wondered, *Will we ever know who did it?* It made him sick.

Wood turned the picture over and read the mimeographed information taped to the back:

JEFFERSON PARISH SHERIFF'S OFFICE
ITEM #E-1377-85 Please Call # 391-1926

Nichole Jarrard Lopatta, W/F, 8 yrs old, DOB: 12/7/77, 733 Carrollwood Village, Apt., #95, Gretna, La.

Ht: 4′, Wt: 63 lbs., long brown straight hair with redish tint, freckles on the nose and she is open and friendly.

CLOTHING: Lt. blue t-shirt Lt. blue pleated skirt Blue flip-flops

Last seen 6/2/85, 4:30 p.m., at Tres Vidas Apts., 733 Carrollwood Village, Gretna, LA.

Wood turned the picture back over. They misspelled reddish. He looked at Nichole's young face and thought of the line ". . . she is open and friendly."

Spade called at that moment.

"Goodbye chiefs. Goodbye Juvenile Division," Spade said.

"Fuckin' A," Wood agreed. "And goodbye to dozens of pages of reports on investigations of bars Jodee Lopatta frequented. And hundreds of almost daily phone calls from every frightened jerk-off east of the Mississippi. Goodbye to the thousands of license plates we've run from the Tres Vidas, the Navy yard, the entire fuckin' West Bank. Goodbye to bogus investigators who couldn't solve shit."

No need for Wood to name names. Spade knew the type.

"Still no word on who authorized having the body cremated?" Spade asked.

"Nope. The coroner didn't. The family didn't. We didn't. Some of the bigwigs think Gibbs made the call, but there's no proof. This case has been so damn screwy. You know we had to kick one guy off the task force. Took it upon himself to pick up Jodee Lopatta in the middle of the night, before one of her early morning interviews, and drive her out to the crime scene to see her reactions."

"Jesus. It's a wonder she hasn't gone off the deep

end."

"He thought Jodee was involved." Wood gave the lame excuse the St. John detective gave when asked why he took Jodee to the crime scene.

"If she was, he woulda tainted the case taking her to the scene."

"Exactly. What a cluster fuck this task force has been."

When Wood paused for a breath, Spade injected, "Thank God the paper hasn't printed that lawyer's name yet."

"It's only a matter of time," Wood said.

"In every homicide case, it's always a matter of time."

Part Three

"I think I just put my ass in the electric chair."

Twenty

Saturday, August 10, 1985.

"It's always a matter of time."

Barry Wood recalled his conversation with Spade as he sat in a stuffy interview room at the Santa Rosa County Sheriff's Department in Florida on a steamy Saturday evening. Also in the room were FBI Special Agents Vic Harvey and Joseph Hummel, as well as Santa Rosa County Detective Corporal Larry Bryant and a lone white female. Bryant was the reason they were there. Bryant had called because the female, thirty-two-year-old Judith Corinne Walters, had been picked up with her boyfriend, John Francis Wille. In interviewing Walters and Wille, Bryant felt these two may have been involved in several murders along the Gulf Coast, including South Louisiana. Bryant had a gut feeling about Wille, a gut feeling about the Lopatta murder and the murder of Billy Phillips.

"I was born in Laurel, Mississippi on January 30, 1953," Judith said, answering the first question put to

215

her after her rights were read and waived.

Wood took notes as Judith detailed her marriage to James Walters and how she'd left James and her son and daughter in 1985 to live with John Francis Wille in Norco, Louisiana. Judith first met Wille in 1983, first had sex with him in 1984, and moved in with him in 1985.

Some time ago, Wille brought up the subject of their having kids. Judith told him she had a hysterectomy several years ago. Wille wanted her to attend a seminar at Tulane University for women having difficulty having children. No matter now she tried to explain to Wille that she could never have children, Wille did not comprehend. He became enraged when she refused to attend the seminar.

In the pursuant argument, Wille became more upset, claiming Judith would implicate him in crimes committed by him in her presence. Judith claimed Wille was insanely jealous and believed she is having sexual relations with anyone who looks at or speaks to her. Wille's jealousy was a source of an unlimited number of heated and violent arguments in which Wille often beat Judith.

Wood stared closely at Judith, at the pockmarked, sunken face, the cold eyes, the long greasy brown hair. Judith told the investigators that Wille was capable of extremely violent acts, many of which she had seen. Wood felt his skin crawling. He knew, deep in his gut, that Larry Bryant was certainly correct in calling Lou-

216

isiana on these guys.

Two days previously, on Thursday, August 8, Wood was on the evening watch at the JPSO Detective Bureau, when he received a call from his headquarters. Dispatcher Ruby told Wood that a *Times-Picayune* reporter was on the phone. Wood answered the line and reporter Bruce Nolan immediately asked if he was part of the Lopatta Task Force.

"Yes, I am."

Then Nolan asked if Wood had any follow-up information on the investigation. Wood referred him to the task force spokesman. Then Nolan asked if Wood had any information, specifically, about the St. John detectives in Florida following the lead on a suspect who'd confessed.

"What?!" Wood was floored. "What suspect? What do you mean, Florida?"

Wood got Nolan off the line quickly and called his chief. Hell, if Wood had known, the newspaperman would have had better luck calling anyone but Wood. Convinced there was a leak in the task force, a leak directly to the paper, Wood had complained bitterly of finding their hard-worked investigative information the following morning in the paper. Someone had to be feeding them. Wood was livid. But he was more shocked at receiving such a call.

Chief Eugene Fields was at home. Wood asked him about the suspect and about St. John detectives in

Florida. Fields said he had no idea.

"I'll call you back," Fields said and hung up.

Fields called back a few minutes later. He was fit to be tied. He confirmed that St. John had detectives in Santa Rosa County, Florida, in Milton specifically. No, he had not learned why they were there exactly. Yes, it was probably connected to the Lopatta case, which enraged Fields. No, they hadn't contacted the task force leaders. They had just gone.

Fields ended the conversation with a curt, "Pack your bags."

The following morning Wood met SA Vic Harvey and Joseph Hummel at a truck stop north of New Orleans in Slidell, Louisiana. Chief Fields had given Wood money and a Sheriff's Office credit card and told him to go. No red tape. No hesitation. Just go.

On their way, Wood and Harvey and Hummel talked about it. Skeptical at first, they wondered what awaited them in Milton. Harvey had even brought his golf clubs. So did Hummel, figuring they were about to get a free vacation along the Florida Gulf Coast. They speculated on what golf courses they could play, since Milton was close to the fair-sized city of Pensacola. The three investigators sped all the way to Florida, averaging about eighty-five miles an hour. Passing several marked police cars along the way, they were never stopped.

Landing in Milton, they checked into a motel. Harvey checked in with the local FBI office. Since they arrived late, they went to dinner. With nothing much to do, Wood studied his buddies. Hummel was a Yankee, a rookie FBI man, with the clean-cut mannerisms that followed in the long tradition of J. Edgar Hoover's handpicked lot. Hummel was stuffy. He often speculated aloud, something an experienced homicide detective never did. Hummel kept throwing up ideas, just to see who would shoot them down. Harvey and Wood did a lot of shooting.

Vic Harvey, on the other hand, was a fifteen-year FBI veteran. At 6', he was in excellent shape, even though he was somewhat balding on the top of his blond head. An old Hoover man, Harvey did not like the liberal turns taken by the new FBI. Harvey was an FBI Tactical Squad member. He had worked several deep undercover operations in Chicago. He also went to Wounded Knee after those FBI agents were murdered.

Married to a secretary in the New Orleans FBI Office, Harvey had two daughters from a previous marriage, daughters he didn't get to see much, since they lived with their mother in a different city.

Wood liked Harvey immediately. Funny, quick with a joke, Harvey told Wood that homicide wasn't his forte. He was still a good investigator and a good interviewer.

* * *

219

The following morning, Saturday, August 10, the three dropped by the FBI resident agent's office and met SA Fred McFaul. The small office, in which five agents worked, looked like a nice assignment to Wood. He noticed that only senior agents got to pull such cushy duty.

Fred McFaul was a large man with a booming voice. Also a fifteen-year FBI veteran, McFaul had built a solid career and a nice home on a hill overlooking Escambia Bay. McFaul told Harvey that they had just missed the St. John detectives who left the previous day.

Wood figured they passed each other on the way to Florida.

McFaul set up a meeting at the Sheriff's Office and shortly Wood and Harvey and Hummel met Larry Bryant at the Santa Rosa Sheriff's Office. Bryant was also a large man, with sandy hair and a deep voice laced with a heavy Southern drawl.

Bryant told them he had contacted the St. John Sheriff's Office after he'd arrested a man from St. John named John Francis Wille on an arson charge. Wille told Bryant he had killed an old woman in La Place. In the course of conversation, Wille hinted about dumped bodies.

Wood's mind worked in overdrive. Wille was from St. John. Dumped bodies? Wille was someone familiar with the area where Nichole was dumped. Wood learned that Wille had confessed to a couple of kill-

220

ings to the St. John detectives, but was recanting those statements.

Bryant felt the St. John detectives arrived unprepared. They didn't even bring a change of clothes, much less money for a place to stay. A Santa Rosa captain pulled some strings to put them up in a nice hotel.

Wille gave the St. John detectives a statement; admitting to committing arson and then beating an elderly neighbor, Ida Boudreaux. Wille said that after he beat Miss Boudreaux, she died of a heart attack. He also admitted to killing a man named Mark in Louisiana, with an accomplice named Joe. They just wanted to scare him. "I had him by the top of his head and shoved him under," Willie said, "and when I went to pull him back up, he wouldn't come back up. It was like Joe was holding him down. And, well, he drowned."

The Lopatta case was not mentioned during the statement. Wille was asked, however, about the case and denied any involvement. The two St. John detectives headed back for Louisiana.

John Francis Wille immediately recanted his murder confession. Larry Bryant was not pursuaded. He told Wood and Harvey that he felt sure Wille was a killer. Bryant had spent more time with Wille than the St. John dicks. Wille would play with them. Wille loved the attention. Then Bryant told them how Wille had tried to burn down a woman's home with alcohol just because he'd been evicted. Wille displayed no conscience or guilt.

The word sociopath came into Wood's mind. If there was one thing Wood felt he knew about Nichole's killer . . . whoever it was . . . was that it was a sociopath, a human void of any conscience.

During the conversation between the FBI agents, Larry Bryant and Barry Wood, Wood learned that Wille's girlfriend Judith Walters was also being held.

"Hey," Wood said, "let's talk to her. Girlfriends usually know the goings-on of their boyfriends."

"I was going to suggest that," Bryant said. He pointed out that Judith and Wille's relationship seemed odd. Beside the fact that she was twelve years his senior, they both seemed . . . eerie.

The investigators had come all the way to Florida. Since Wille did not want to talk anymore, why not talk to Judith?

As soon as Wood and the FBI agents began interviewing Judith Walters, they realized that the golf clubs in their trunk would go unused.

After some initial questions about Judith's background and her relationship with Wille, Vic Harvey found Judith to be resistant to specific questions.

Larry Bryant pulled Wood outside the interview room. He told Wood how Wille had been communicating with Judith through jail-house notes. Bryant had been studying Judith closely. He said, "I believe she knows something about the little girl's murder and knows that's what you're leading up to." He said it was a gut feeling. Wood smiled. Homicide dicks often went on gut instinct. Sometimes, it paid off.

Bryant suggested, since he had a rapport with Judith, that he take over the initial questioning. Wood and Hummel and Harvey agreed. Bryant led the way back into the tiny interview room. Instead of sitting across from Judith, as SA Harvey had, Bryant sat next to her, close to her. He spoke to her, in his slow Southern drawl, not like a detective, but like a good-old-boy, a friend, someone she could release her guilt to, someone to confide in.

Wood could see Judith relaxing slowly. She was read her rights once again before the serious questioning started. And there, in the confines of the tiny room, Judith painted a vivid, horrifying picture for the four men.

Beginning on the date of May 31, Judith documented her and Wille's traveling in her 1976 white Chevrolet Impala to Milton, Florida, then to Pensacola. Arguing and drinking Southern Comfort and Coke, Wille finally switched to tequila. Judith became drunk and found later that she was in Biloxi, Mississippi. It was early on the morning of Saturday, June 1, 1985. Wille told her he was taking her to Norco, Louisiana. Judith said that Wille was beginning to act very strange and based on past experiences, she felt something "terrible was about to happen."

223

Judith said as they approached the twin span bridges in Slidell, Louisiana, Wille screamed, "Hey, I know that guy," referring to a hitchhiker on Interstate 10 westbound. Wille drove all the way to the twin spans, made a U-turn, then traveled eastbound to the first Slidell exit to pull another U-turn so that he could pick up the hitchhiker.

Based on the conversation between Wille and the hitchhiker, concerning mutual friends, it did appear that Wille knew the hitchhiker personally. Judith did not get a good look at the hitchhiker as he entered the vehicle and was only able to state that the hitchhiker was a white male. Judith said that based on the fact that the sun was so bright and hot, it had to be early Saturday morning. After picking up the hitchhiker they continued toward New Orleans.

When Judith next woke up, it was the afternoon or early evening of Sunday, June 2, 1985, and they were parked in a residential neighborhood. Judith remembers sitting up and noticing trees and several power lines. Judith said that Wille subsequently told her that the neighborhood they had been parked in was Terrytown, Gretna, Louisiana. She said that she and Wille had been in Terrytown on one other occasion prior to June 2.

Judith said that Wille got back in the car alone, placed her head on his lap and proceeded to drive away. She said that after traveling only a couple of blocks, Wille pulled over, parked the car and got out.

She is sure that they were still in the same residential area because they had only traveled one or two blocks before stopping. Once he was out of the car Wille walked to the front of the vehicle and leaned against the driver's side front fender. She is sure that Wille remained by the vehicle because of the fact she felt the car move when he leaned against it and it never moved again to indicate Wille left the side of the car. Judith said that they were only there a couple of minutes when she heard several children playing nearby.

The next thing she heard was Wille saying, "Aren't you a pretty one. Who do you take after, your mommy or your daddy?" and in the same breath said, "What were you doing that took so long?" as if speaking to two different people who had approached the vehicle together. Judith said that after hearing Wille speak to the young child and the other individual, she again fell asleep. Judith was next awakened by someone kicking the back of her seat. She said that it was not like an adult kicking the seat but more like a child. Judith sat up and turned around to see who was kicking her seat. When she looked in the back she saw the hitchhiker that they had picked up sitting next to a white female, approximately seven years of age.

Judith was shown a photograph of Nichole Michelle Lopatta, and she positively identified her as the child seated in the backseat of her vehicle.

Barry Wood felt himself gulp loudly. *This was it,* he told himself. *This was going to be the beginning of*

225

the end.

Nichole's photograph was initialed by SA Harvey and Judith and placed in an envelope. Judith explained that Wille refused to tell her who the little girl was, where she had come from, or where they were going. Judith said that she knew something terrible was about to happen because Wille had started drinking the tequila again. Judith continued to ask Wille what she had done to make him angry and was only told that "It's not what you've done, it's what you haven't done." He then told her that "One day you will learn not to upset me, one day you'll learn."

Wille drove on River Road in La Place, Louisiana, to the Little Gypsy Power Plant. By now it is dark and the power plant lights illuminated the sky. She said that Wille had begun to act very strange and was extremely upset so she stopped questioning him about the little girl. Wille got on the Interstate (I-55) in La Place, Louisiana, and headed toward Hammond, Louisiana, northbound. Wille exited the Interstate, made a U-turn, and headed back to La Place, Louisiana, stopping at an Exxon station to use the bathroom. Judith said that while Wille used the station's bathroom, she remained in the car with the little girl and the hitchhiker. Judith said that no one spoke while at the Exxon station, not even the little girl. She said that when Wille returned to the car he became extremely irate and began accusing her of eyeing the hitchhiker and wanting to go to bed with him (the

226

hitchhiker). Wille drove from the Exxon station and entered the "old highway" (Highway 51). Wille had purchased a Coke at the Exxon station so Judith started drinking again. Wille drove for a short time traveling northbound, and then pulled off to the side of the road and parked the vehicle. Judith said that she started to exit the car when Wille jumped out of the driver's side door, ran around to the passenger side, and slammed the door.

Wille grabbed her hand and started walking toward the water after telling the hitchhiker, "We'll be right back." Judith said that at this time she overheard the little girl ask, "Where's my mommy?" Judith said that she then overheard the hitchhiker and little girl singing a song. Judith said that Wille accompanied her to the water's edge where they sat down.

She attempted to talk to Wille but he continued to rant and rave, until he suddenly calmed down and began discussing his family. He talked about how he thought that his mother and sister never really understood him and how they had abandoned him. Judith said that she attempted to reason with him by telling him not to worry about the past but to instead "think about now." That statement seemed to incense Wille. He jumped up and began beating Judith with his fist. Judith said that she just lay there not even fighting back since she knew from past physical beating inflicted by Wille upon her that it was useless to resist. Wille accused Judith of wanting to leave him just like

227

everyone else and wanting to have sex with the hitch-hiker. She said that she was now positive that something terrible was about to happen because horrible things always happen when Wille got like this. She had seen Wille commit numerous violent acts, including murder, when he was in a similar mood.

Judith said that after Wille stopped beating her he returned to the car, leaving her by the water. Wille sat in the car for a few moments, then drove off with the child and the hitchhiker, leaving Judith behind. Judith said that she remained there for approximately one hour and a half, drinking and crying.

Judith said that just as Wille was returning, a second car was stopping approximately two hundred yards down the road. The driver and passenger in the second vehicle exchanged places and drove off. When Wille got out of the car he was alone and immediately accused Judith of having sex with the occupants of the second vehicle.

Wille told Judith, "if you think you can screw around on me, I'll make sure you'll never do it again." Judith said at this time Wille jumped into the water. When he got out of the water, he demanded to know what exactly Judith and the hitchhiker had discussed while he was in the bathroom at the Exxon station. No matter how vehemently Judith denied speaking to or flirting with the hitchhiker, Wille continued to get madder and madder. Judith said that Wille suddenly started to laugh and said "I don't have to worry about you screwing up with him." Judith said that she again asked where the hitchhiker and the little girl were, which only enraged Wille further. Judith said that Wille dragged her to the car and drove a short distance only to pull off the road and park again.

Judith said it was pitch-black out as Wille dragged her from the car by her hair, all the while attempting to get something out of his pocket. Wille kept saying, "If you had only kept your mouth shut and not made me mad." Wille threw her to the ground and told her he would show her exactly where the hitchhiker was. Still dragging Judith by her hair, Wille pulled a cigarette lighter out of his pocket. Stopping, Wille lit the lighter and told Judith to look. She looked and saw something so mutilated, she couldn't recognize it. The lighter went out. Wille relit it and moved closer. Judith saw the mutilated body of the hitchhiker.

Wille, still pulling Judith's hair, shoved her face down to within an inch of the hitchhiker's groin. Wille growled, "Tell me you want to screw that. What are you gonna do with a man who ain't got a dick?" Judith begged Wille to stop. She saw there was nothing left of the man's groin. Her face was so close, she got blood on her.

"You see the hand that touched your body?" Wille asked.

Judith looked and the man's hand was gone. The other hand was mutilated as well. Wille threw her down and beat her. She tried to get up. Wille pulled

229

her back down and made love to her right there next to the hitchhiker's body. After, Judith heard a splash as if Wille had thrown the hitchhiker's body into the water. Judith said she was hysterical, but fought it. The two climbed back in the Chevy. Wille remained calm. Based on past experiences, she expected Wille to remain calm.

Wille suddenly started screaming and drove off with Judith. They drove a short distance. Wille got out, pulled her out by the hair, took out the lighter, and showed her something. Wille yanked her hair so hard, he pulled some out. This made him angrier. Judith knew he wanted her to see the little girl's dead body. She tried not to look. Wille grabbed Judith's hand and placed it on something. It felt cold. Judith knew she was touching the girl's leg. Wille jerked Judith back and forth and said, "If you just do what I tell you, everything would be okay, but you always upset me, so you have to pay for it."

After Wille threatened to kill Judith's husband and son, Judith looked at the body. She could tell the girl was dead. Wille let go of Judith's hair. Judith sat down, turned her back to the body and cried. She heard Wille breathing heavily a few minutes later, turned and saw him. "He was raping the dead child." Wille spent at least five minutes doing that.

After, Wille stood up and told Judith, "Are you ready to go? Are you hungry? How about something to eat?" Wille was talking as if he'd been out shopping, not like he'd just murdered and raped.

Judith said she wasn't hungry, but wanted to wash up. She was covered with blood. They walked to the car arm in arm. At the car, Wille smoked a cigarette. They then drove to an Ecol Truck Stop where Judith washed the blood from her hair and hands. She was unable to get the blood out of her shirt and pants.

They drove to a Popeye's Chicken outlet on Williams Boulevard in Kenner, Louisiana, to get something to eat. At Popeye's Wille was waited on by a black female. He asked for an empty bag in addition to their food. Back in the car, Wille pulled something from the backseat and put it in the empty bag. Whatever it was, it was bloody.

Wille drove home to Milton, Florida, arriving in Milton early Monday morning, June 3. They returned to Norco in mid-June. Wille and Judith got into a heated argument over the Lopatta murder. The argument branched out into their sexual habits. Wille complained again that Judith would not perform oral sex with him. Judith asked Wille outright if he had murdered the little girl or the hitchhiker.

Wille said, "I don't need help handling any woman, big or little." Wille went on claiming that if Judith wouldn't give him oral sex, he'd get it elsewhere. He claimed he got the little girl to do it. Wille described the murder of Nichole Lopatta to Judith in detail.

Barry Wood, listening quietly, felt his stomach bottom out with the description of the killing. It was pitiful. As Judith described Wille's acts in detail, the striking of the little girl, the strangling, the raping, Wood remained unemotional. He concentrated on listening, seeking clues in Judith's story, clues that could corroborate the story, the sickening story.

Judith said that the only time she heard the little girl speak was when she overheard the child singing and when she asked for her mother.

". . . when she asked for her mother." The words were like a slap to Wood's face. *Jesus Christ! These were not people. They were monsters.*

Judith went on to elaborate about a *Penthouse* magazine which contained an article on Henry Lee Lucas. Wille considered Lucas a god, someone to look up to. Judith remembered that when Wille kidnapped the little girl on June 2, there were several pieces of pornographic material in the trunk of the Chevy, material Wille disposed of at the scene of the child's murder. Judith wasn't sure, but there may have been a copy of the *Penthouse* with the Lucas article among the material.

Judith said there was a possibility that Wille kept a diary which would detail his numerous violent acts. If there was a diary, it would be at Wille's home in Norco.

Judith added that Wille once made the statement that he had learned in prison that the best defense to a crime was the insanity defense. He learned it reading a law book.

232

At the conclusion of Judith's initial statement, she was taken back to her jail cell. Wood, Larry Bryant, and Special Agents Harvey and Hummel discussed what they just heard. Talking slowly and surely, moving almost in slow motion, the men seemed to be stunned by the magnitude of what they just heard.

"There's more," someone said.

"She's not telling us everything."

"More murders, I mean."

Everyone agreed that Judith had held back. There was more to the story. Wood could only imagine how much worse it could get. Certainly there could be more murders.

Wood felt he'd just endured a torture session, listening to this heinous murder. How could a mother of two allow this to happen in her presence? Wood felt relieved that the information would finally bring an end to the long, tedious investigation, that he had finally learned who had killed Nichole. But he knew the long journey was far from over. There was still a lot of work to do. In the movies, murder cases ended at this point sometimes. In real life, it went on and on.

Wood stood and stretched and headed for the nearest phone. He had to call home. The case was broken, thanks to Larry Bryant. Wood noted that it was Bryant who could read Judith Walters. During the interview, when Walters was holding back, she tried to hide her eyes. Bryant would immediately ease her

233

around to get to the truth, to free Judith of the guilty feelings she had bottled inside.

Wood remembered Bryant's chilling postscript. "She's still holding back."

Wood called Chief Fields immediately. When the chief got on the line, Wood told him, "Well, we got Nichole's killers here."

"What was that?"

"We just solved the Nichole Lopatta murder."

Fields sounded surprised. "You didn't see the morning paper," he told Wood. "The St. John detectives don't think Wille killed anybody. They interviewed him."

"They interviewed the wrong person. They should have talked to Wille's girlfriend."

Wood could hear Fields writing something. "So the killer was John Wille, right? You sure?"

"Judith told us things that only the murderers would know. Specific things. You ought to hear the things that Wille did to Nichole and how Judith watched. It's worse than sick." Wood took in a deep breath and continued. "John Francis Wille killed Nichole Lopatta, but that ain't all. Billy Phillips was also in on Nichole's kidnapping and murder. Then Wille killed Phillips."

"Then the bodies were connected after all," Fields said.

Wood smiled to himself. He smiled for himself and the other homicide dicks *who knew the bodies had to*

234

be connected.

"We didn't mention Phillips to her at all. She upped with the information on her own. It's all connected."

"Good job," Fields said. Then he told Wood that he would now have to tell Sheriff Lee and then figure how to release the news to the public without stepping on anybody's dick in St. John.

Hanging up, Wood took in a deep breath. He felt a great relief.

Later that night, while trying to sleep in a strange motel room, Wood had trouble. Whatever relief he'd felt had dissipated. Everytime he closed his eyes, he saw Nichole's smiling face; then he saw a hand striking it. And he saw, like a macabre death-play, the little girl's murder at the hands of a . . . monster.

He knew they had better get enough details from Judith to corroborate her story. Then Wood thought of Norman Gibbs. The man was certainly innocent of Nichole's murder, but Wood felt no remorse for the lawyer, for the heat put on him. Wood believed Gibbs was a child molester. He probably molested Nichole and other little girls.

Lying awake in bed, Wood tried to cheer himself up with thoughts of a newspaper article he was dying to read, the article that said Wille hadn't done it.

Way to go . . . news media. Wrong again!

The article in that morning's *Times-Picayune* was titled, "La Place murder confessions discounted."

235

The article began with a statement. There was no evidence linking a La Place man to three area killings in the past two years, despite his confessions. Quoting St. John detectives, the paper went on to say that John Francis Wille, twenty-one, had told police he'd killed six people in Louisiana, Texas, and Florida, including three in the La Place area. Citing no physical evidence and facts that did not match what police knew of the crimes, Captain Joe Oubre discounted the confession.

The paper went on about how Wille grew up on East Eleventh Street in La Place, across the street from the residence of St. John Sheriff Lloyd Johnson.

Santa Rosa detectives claimed that Wille told them he drowned a man in a bayou near La Place, leading them to suspect he might be responsible for the murder of Billy Phillips, whose body was found near that of Nichole Lopatta on the same day. Wille also confessed to murdering Ida Boudreaux, seventy-seven, and setting fire to her house. Wille also confessed to killing a man in 1983.

St. John authorities were being careful. They said they didn't want to end up in the same situation as with Henry Lee Lucas, a man who confessed to 350 murders, most of which were bogus.

The paper's article concluded with facts about Wille's past, how he dropped out of East St. John High School, how he had a minor criminal record as an adult in St. John and St. Charles Parishes for battery and trespassing.

The paper went on to directly quote neighbors.

"He was just another normal kid in the neighborhood."

"He was a funny kid at times. Not smart-alecky, but just strange."

"He's very pleasant, very polite, and very neat. I was never aware of any problems with him."

Twenty-one

Sunday, August 11, 1985.

The Times-Picayune article the following day had a different tone to it. "Drifter may face slaying rap," was the title. Unlike the previous day's news report, which was by a *Times-Picayune* reporter, this article came off the UPI wire service.

Reporting from Milton, the article said the bizarre case of a Louisiana drifter, who confessed to murders in three states, then denied them, took another twist when lawmen, searching his apartment, found bloodstained clothing.

Larry Bryant of the Santa Rosa County Sheriff's Office now believed a case reported as a hit-and-run was actually a murder perpetrated by John Francis Wille. Bryant claimed that Wille had been positively linked to five murders, including three in Louisiana.

St. John The Baptist Parish authorities, however, still maintained there was no evidence linking Wille

238

to any murders in their jurisdiction.

"I can't speak for the state of Louisiana," a kind hearted Bryant was quoted as saying, "but I'm sure it's just like what we've got here. We've got so much that it's going to take a long time to pull it all together."

Asked if Wille might be charged in the Louisiana cases, Bryant flatly said, "If it was here, I would."

The case Bryant was working on was that of Frank Powe, killed on July 15. Powe's body, run over several times, was found on I-10 near Milton.

Bryant said he'd linked Wille to the murders of Billy Phillips, Ida Boudreaux and a girl Bryant identified as Cathy, whose beaten body was found in a drainage ditch two months earlier. Wille was also being questioned about other Louisiana murders, the deaths of a black prostitute, and two people called "Mark and Joe."

Spade read the article carefully. He had tried calling Wood the previous day, when the first Wille article hit the paper, and found that his friend was in Florida. Spade envied him, being where the action was. Reading between the lines of the articles, Spade felt Wood and his buddies just may have found their man. If Wille murdered Billy Phillips, he murdered Nichole Lopatta. Spade's homicide instincts were certain of that. "A good homicide man doesn't believe in coincidence." The bodies *had* to be connected.

A "drifter"; the paper described Wille as a drifter. It sounded logical, a traveling criminal. Worse actually. Wille sounded like a traveling serial killer.

Back at the Santa Rosa Jail, Barry Wood and SA Hummel met John Francis Wille. Wood immediately noticed two things about the man. The protruding brow and the sneering smile on his face.

They met Wille in the booking section of the jail where Wille had been brought to be fingerprinted by Wood and Hummel. The prints the detectives needed went beyond the usual rolled fingers. They rigged a coffee can with a fingerprint card taped to it in order to get prints of Wille's complete hand, palm, everything.

Wille seemed amused at the somewhat awkward method. He was also amused as they took color Polaroids. Wood discovered, when they told Wille exactly who they were, that Wille disliked the FBI, but was friendly to Wood, who was from a Sheriff's Office. Wille said he liked deputies and had lived across the street from the sheriff of St. John Parish.

Monday, August 12, 1985.

When interviewed by FBI Special Agents Frederick McFaul and Michael Dill at the Santa Rosa

Jail, Judith Walters was asked to determine the whereabouts and activities of John Francis Wille during the latter part of March 1985. According to Judith, Wille traveled to Pensacola between March 15 and March 24.

When asked about Wille being in the Fort Walton Beach, Florida area, Judith said that while she and Wille lived in Milton in June of 1985, Wille told her about a trip he made to Fort Walton Beach during mid-June.

The investigators asked about a different murder case this day. A case in Fort Walton. Judith provided no useful information relative to that case.

The same day, SA McFaul and SA Dill, along with Okaloosa County Sheriff's Investigator Don Vinson, interviewed John Francis Wille at the Santa Rosa Jail. Wille, dressed in dark prison clothes, his oily hair messed and curly, wore a thin moustache. A smirk on his face, Wille waived his rights and agreed to be interviewed. Wille was a powerfully built man, about 5′11″ tall, weighing 175 pounds. He had a square jaw, brown eyes, and a wide nose.

Wille was questioned about the murder of Tommie Whiddon, whose body was found on a section of beach of the Eglin Air Force Base Reservation, Fort Walton Beach, Florida on March 27, 1985.

Wille said he was not in Fort Walton in March 1985.

"I didn't kill anybody in Fort Walton Beach," he said, the smirk still on his face.

During the questioning, Wille also volunteered that he did not kill Nichole Lopatta. At the end of the questioning, Wille said he had not killed anyone and blamed the authorities for trying to make a big deal about his arrest.

On the way back to New Orleans, Wood went over his case notes. Coming across *The Times-Picayune* article about all the bodies dumped in St. Charles and St. John Parishes, he put marks next to four names. Besides Nichole Lopatta and Billy Phillips, they had reason to strongly suspect Wille was directly involved in the murders of Donald Ferraro of Jefferson Parish, who was found stabbed and shot to death in 1984; and Kathy L. Mickenheim, found drowned after being struck on the head. He wondered if Wille could be linked to any of the other twenty-one bodies.

Upon arriving at the FBI office Monday morning, Wood and Harvey debriefed everyone about Wille and Judith. The immediate course of action for the members was to corroborate as much of Judith's story as possible. Teams were sent back to the crime scene to look under the I-10 overpass at Highway 51, where Judith said Nichole's murder actually took place.

Photographic lineups were compiled with Judith's photo and Wille's Polaroids.

Tuesday, August 13, 1985.

Spade was sure the Lopatta case was broken when he read between the lines of the latest article in *The Times-Picayune.* "La Place man is probed in more murders" was the title of the article that named Wille as a suspect in Nichole's murder. According to the paper, a JPSO detective and two FBI special agents questioned Wille over the weekend about the Lopatta case. Spade skimmed the rest of the article, which linked Wille to other murders in Louisiana and Florida.

When Barry Wood called later that day, Spade's strong suspicion was confirmed.

"You're not going to believe how it went down," Wood said. "I'll tell you later. Man, they massacred that little girl." Wood sounded tired and distant. Spade knew the feeling.

* * *

Wednesday, August 14, 1985.

Upon returning to the detective office, Barry Wood was assaulted by detectives wanting to know about Judith and Wille. He kept his explanations short. He was happy to receive an immediate assignment. Before leaving, however, he was passed an envelope mailed to Sheriff Harry Lee earlier that day. The note inside read:

Harry Lee, Sheriff
Jefferson Parish, 200 Huey P. Long St.,
Gretna, La.

For your information JOHN FRANCIS WILLE is the murderer of Nichole Lopatta.

One Who Knows.

Wood put the note in his case file on his way out. He spent the better part of the day verifying one aspect of Judith's story. According to Judith, her fourteen-year-old daughter Sheila Walters had befriended and picked up a juvenile boy, sixteen, in May 1985. Judith and Wille and Sheila and the boy had been together over a weekend. When Wood interviewed the boy, now seventeen, his story was extremely close to Judith's story.

244

The boy obviously had no knowledge of or connection to Wille's violent acts.

Wood was happy to have verified that part of Judith's story and to find the boy alive. Judith thought that Wille might have killed the boy before they left town. The more truth they could attribute to Judith Walters, the closer John Francis Wille came to the electric chair.

Barry Wood went by the Popeye's in Kenner and talked to the manager, learning the names of the people who worked the store on June 2. He took down the names and said he'd be back to interview them. Wood never told the manager what he was working on, only that he needed to speak to the employees about an important matter they might have witnessed.

That same day St. Charles Sheriff's Office detectives verified other parts of Judith's story, interviewing Judith's estranged husband and eleven-year-old son. Neither had any knowledge of the killings, but both verified the details of Judith's travels with John Francis Wille.

Also, on the same day, FBI SA Vic Harvey, accompanied by JPSO Detective Patricia Montecino, met and interviewed Judith's daughter, Sheila Renee Walters, fourteen. At Sheila's grandmother's residence, and in the presence of the grandmother, Sheila talked to the investigators. Before the interview began, the investigators explained that Sheila was considered a witness, not a suspect.

At the inception of the interview, SA Harvey showed Sheila a Polaroid photograph of John Francis Wille, received by SA Harvey on October 10, 1985, at Milton, Florida. Upon examining it, Sheila responded that she was familiar with this individual and knew him to be the boyfriend of her mother, Judith Corinne Walters. Sheila said she first met Wille during the summer of 1984 when her mother drove her to the post office in Norco, Louisiana, and they met Wille. She stated that her mother, upon seeing Wille on this occasion, began kissing him in the post office and told Sheila that this was her boyfriend.

Sheila said that on or about May 12, 1985, her mother came to her and said that Wille had just stolen $3,000 from his grandfather, and they, Sheila and her mother and Wille, were getting out of town. Her mother advised that of the $3,000 Wille had used about $500 to buy a gun from a store, thought by Sheila to be in the Norco area. She said all three of them got in her mother's car and drove to New Orleans where they stayed at the Metairie Inn on Airline Highway, with Sheila in a separate but adjoining room with that of her mother and

Wille.

Sheila said that upon arrival in Milton, Florida, they resided for several weeks at the Thrifty Motel in Milton. Again she had a room to herself, and Wille and her mother had an adjoining or nearby room.

She said that he often wore a shoulder holster but did not have the gun in it on most occasions.

Wille practiced nearly every day in the back of the lot with the pistol.

Sheila was asked if her mother had any boyfriends other than Wille, and she remarked that her mother who often drank very heavily had slept with several different men.

Sheila was asked if she was familiar with a Kathy who was from the Norco area and could possibly have been an associate of her mother and/or Wille. She stated that she did not personally know anyone named Kathy but did recall a Kathy whose body was found in the Bonnet Carre Spillway and that she recalled this individual to have a tattoo of "Fred" on her arm. The investigators said they believed this individual to be in fact named Kathy and asked Sheila to give them any information she might have about her.

Sheila replied that the night prior to the discovery of Kathy's body, she and her mother had gone to the Bonnet Carre Spillway to visit Wille who was

247

residing in an orange tent. She said that Wille's tent was approximately ten to twenty feet from where Kathy's body was subsequently found.

Sheila advised that she recalled that Wille always carried a large brown folding-type knife with him and kept his things in a dark blue gym bag with a shoulder strap. She said that Wille attempted to make love to her, on numerous occasions, especially when her mother was drunk, but she would not let him.

Over hot coffee, in a corner of Morning Call Coffee Stand, Wood told Spade the grisly details of Judith's confession. But first he had to tell Spade how they broke the case.

"Hell, we brought our golf clubs."

"What?"

Wood explained that he and the FBI men figured they caught a free trip to the Gulf Coast, why not take in a little R&R. That was until they met Larry Bryant.

"Bryant had Wille and Judith in jail on one of their murders and started talking to both. Wille kept acting sly. He even tried conning the St. John dicks. But it was Judith. She was the key. She was the weak link. When St. John got there, they interviewed Wille instead of Judith. But Bryant steered us to Judith. It didn't take long." Wood didn't add the fact that he had been the first to mention interviewing Judith. Bryant had already thought it. For the next ten minutes, Wood ran down the events: how Nichole was snatched, raped, and murdered; how Wille then murdered Phillips. "But she ain't boned up to everything," Wood concluded. "She's still holding something back. Something probably even more grotesque."

"Jesus!"

Spade lifted his coffee cup in a toast, a sad toast. "Well, here's to good police work."

Wood tapped his cup against his friend's. It was good police work. In spite of the monkey-house task force, it took an observant cop in another state, a cop who paid attention to teletypes and recent events to put two and two together.

Spade was more blunt. "No fuckin' psychic. No psychological profile. No fuckin' polygraph. Just good street police work. A well-informed cop sniffing out a rat."

"All the way back home," Wood said, "I kept remembering those news articles quoting task force sources, 'Girl likely knew brutal killer well.' I kept thinking about that goddamn psychological profile and how it fit Jodee's lawyer friend like a glove."

Wood let out a long, tired sigh. He knew it wasn't over. It was far from over. A homicide case was like

249

a giant jigsaw puzzle. There were so many more pieces to put into place. They were still a long way from strapping John Francis Wille into "Old Sparky," Louisiana's timeworn electric chair in the swampy backwaters of West Feliciana Parish at Angola State Penitentiary.

"I went over the vaunted psychological profile compiled by those FBI specialists last night," Wood said. "Of the fourteen points in the profile, ten aren't even close to fitting Wille or Phillips."

Spade added another old New Orleans homicide cliché, "Every time you try to pull rabbits out of hats, you usually end up with a handful of rabbit shit."

Twenty-two

Thursday, August 15, 1985.

On the two hundred and sixteenth anniversary of the birth of the Emperor Napoleon, a day that is celebrated in south Louisiana with quiet reverence (along with the birthdays of Robert E. Lee and Huey P. Long), Judith Walters was questioned again at the Santa Rosa Jail. Larry Bryant, along with FBI Special Agent Fred McFaul, interviewed Judith, after Judith waived her rights again.

Judith began the statement with the fact that she believed her boyfriend John Francis Wille was bisexual. She provided them with the name and telephone number of a Pensacola man whom she believed had a homosexual relationship with Wille. She also provided similar information on a man in Norco, Louisiana. Judith added some illuminating details about how Wille hated her husband.

Then Judith detailed the kidnapping and death of

251

Nichole Lopatta to investigators. Her statement was basically consistent with her previous statement. This time she was shown a photographic lineup of six black-and-white photos of six white males. She picked out a photo of Billy Phillips, identifying him as the hitchhiker. She explained how they picked up Phillips and how Phillips and Wille "showed up at their car with the little girl," referring to the abduction of Nichole.

After the interview, Bryant and McFaul agreed that Judith was holding something back.

Meanwhile, Santa Rosa officers continued the long process of collecting physical evidence from Judith's Chevy, from Wille's apartment, as well as from Judith and Wille, including hair samples.

Wille and Judith signed "Consent to Search" forms in order for their hair to be taken. Curiously, Wille's signature on the consent form looked like a spiderweb. In comparison to an application for employment Wille filled out on July 29, 1985, in which Wille's signature was legible, the latest version was eerie, to say the least.

Back in New Orleans, Barry Wood learned that the Nichole Lopatta Task Force had been reinstated.

He was included in the list of seventeen officers, this time including Larry Bryant, a St. John Parish Assistant District Attorney, FBI special agents from the Pensacola Field Office, as well as New Orleans FBI agents, and officers from St. John, Jefferson, and St. Charles Parishes. Although the original task force was organized, this second version was so well focused that it impressed Wood.

Three hours later, Wood was sitting in the Kenner Police Station with a tape recorder ready to take a statement from Popeye's employee Debra Davis. He had located the thin, petite woman at her place of employment. Walking into Popeye's, he identified himself and asked Debra if she remembered the evening of June 2. To his surprise, she immediately responded that she did.

"Why?"

It was the first night Debra was promoted to cashier. She went on to say she remembered a man coming in and asking for an empty paper bag. She handed him one, but he wanted a larger one. So she gave him their largest bag, a twenty-five pounder.

Wood began, "The subject being interviewed today is Mrs. Debra Davis. Right now when we're taping this interview, do you have any idea what you're giving this statement in reference to?"

"No."

"Were you working at that Popeye's Fried Chicken

253

place on June the second, 1985?" Wood asked.

Debra said, "Yes."

"And what shift were you working?" Wood said.

"Ah, seven o'clock to eleven o'clock," Debra said.

"Came in early," Wood said.

"Uh huh."

Wood asked, "You stayed until when?"

"12:30 A.M.," Debra answered.

"Okay, what time does the business close to customers?" Wood asked.

"11:00 P.M."

"And is there any way that after 11:00 P.M. you'll occasionally let customers in if there's maybe chicken left over if they come in?" Wood said.

"No."

"So at eleven o'clock, the doors are closed," Wood asked.

"Yes."

"The reason you stayed at 12:30 A.M. was for clean up and to check out and what not?" Wood said.

"Yes, sir," Debra said.

Wood said, "On June the second, do you recall a man and a woman entering the Popeye's some time during your shift and asking for anything in particular? I know we talked about this before. I primarily asked you if you remembered anyone asking for a paper bag. Is that correct?"

254

"Yes."

"Did I give you any other details other than that as far as what he . . . what I was asking you questions about?" Wood said.

"No," Debra said.

"So everything you're about to tell me I did not place in your mind or suggest any details to you. Is that correct?" Wood asked.

Debra said, "True."

"Okay. Tell me what you told me yesterday when we talked and I asked you about a man on June the second that may have come in and asked for a bag. Start from the beginning when you first saw him." Wood said.

"Well he came in and he ordered two pieces of . . . he ordered some chicken, and then he went to the back and he asked me for a bag. I was going to give him a small bag and he asked for a large bag, and he walked out the door, and put something in the bag and put that bag in the garbage can. I don't know what garbage can it was . . ." Debra said.

"Do you recall what time he may have come in?" Wood asked.

"It was after seven o'clock, close to eight o'clock," Debra said.

"Was it dark at that time?" Wood asked.

"Yes."

"So, could it have been after eight o'clock then

since it was dark?" Wood said.

Debra said, "It could have been."

Wood asked, "Could you see anything outside?"

"No."

"Now you said that he put something in the bag. Do you know what he may have put in the bag?" Wood said.

"No."

"Did you see him put anything in the bag?"

"I saw him put something in the bag but I couldn't tell what it was," Debra said.

Wood said, "And where did he put something in the bag? What . . ."

"It was by his car," Debra said.

"By his car?" Wood asked.

"Uh huh."

"Could you tell what part of the car or what he was doing around the car?" Wood said.

"No. He just opened the door, and put something in his bag, and closed the door, and then walked to the garbage can," Debra said.

"Was it the front door, passenger's doors, the back door, or what?" Wood asked.

"No. It's the front on the driver's side," Debra said.

Wood said, "He opened the front door on the driver's side."

"Uh huh."

256

"Did he go into the car first and then come out?" Wood asked.

Debra said, "No. He just put his head in. He put something in the bag and came back out."

Wood then referred to the photos that Davis had identified as Wille and Judith.

"Did I prompt you or give you any kind of hint or give you any information to help you decide who you might have seen that night?" Wood asked.

"No."

Wood said, "So you picked these photographs totally on your own?"

"Yes," Debra said.

The interview was then concluded. Wood had exactly what he wanted, more verification of Judith's statement. And he was sure he now knew what happened to Billy Phillips's missing hand.

When he told Debra whom she had just identified, that these were the killers of Nichole Lopatta, the young woman said, "Oh, my God!" Debra became very nervous. He didn't tell her that the bag she saw Wille throw away contained a human hand. She was too nice a girl to know all the gory details.

Back at the task force, Vic Harvey was elated with Debra Davis's revelations. It was the first bit of concrete information that validated Judith's statements. "If Judith's telling the truth about this, then she's telling the truth about all of it," was the task

257

force consensus.

Wood and Harvey still felt that it wasn't the entire truth.

Sunday, August 18, 1985.

At the Santa Rosa Jail, Judith Walters was reinterviewed by FBI Special Agents Terry Scott and Harry Peel. She acknowledged that she omitted some information in her original statements concerning the murder of Nichole Lopatta. Judith was asked to elaborate, and she did.

She began with the statement that the little girl did not seem to be afraid or upset at the beginning, when they were all in the car. Judith recalled it was very dark outside. Judith asked Wille about the little girl and Wille became very upset. After pulling off Highway 51 north of La Place, a little south of I-55, Wille stopped the Chevy and pulled Judith from the car. Wille jumped in the water, then beat Judith, and left her for an hour. Wille returned in the Chevy with the hitchhiker and the little girl. They drove off in a northerly direction. Pulling off Highway 51 again, Wille continued his beating of Judith until she passed out.

Judith was awakened by noises the little girl was making from the backseat. Then, in a deep cold

258

voice, Judith described the gruesome details of the rape and murder of Nichole Lopatta. The agents took careful notes, doing their best to let their faces remain calm.

The hitchhiker and Wille simultaneously attacked the little girl. During the attack, Wille reached up and pulled Judith over and attempted to get Judith to perform oral sex on him. Judith became sick, which made Wille angrier. He went back to his sexual attack on the girl.

Judith witnessed Wille choke the girl to death, then watched as both men continued their sexual attacks on the dead body. Even after the girl was obviously dead, the two men beat her brutally with their hands.

The hitchhiker moved to Judith and forced Judith to perform oral sex on him. Wille told Judith she'd better do it right. After a few moments, the hitchhiker withdrew from Judith saying that she wasn't doing it right. The hitchhiker went back to attacking the dead girl's body with Wille.

Some minutes later, while Wille was still attacking the dead body, the hitchhiker went behind Wille, inserted his penis into Wille's anus and screwed Wille. When the men finished, they climbed out of the car.

Judith said, "I felt sorry for the little girl." She attempted to cover the body with newspapers, but

Wille became enraged and pulled the papers off the body.

Wille climbed into the front seat with Phillips and Judith and drove off, the body still on the backseat. Judith could see Wille was enraged. He stopped the car and made the hitchhiker get out. After speeding off, Judith asked Wille why he had kicked the hitchhiker out, which made him even angrier, if that was possible. He stomped the brakes and kicked Judith out.

She wound up walking for a while with the hitchhiker. After a while, Judith had to go to the bathroom and went off in the bushes. As she was pulling up her pants, she was confronted by Wille, who demanded to know what she and the hitchhiker had been doing. Wille struck Judith, knocking her to the ground. She saw the hitchhiker now and he told Wille to leave Judith alone, that nothing had gone on between them. When the hitchhiker got close to Wille, Wille struck him in the stomach or chest (Judith wasn't sure). Instantly blood squirted, "all over the place." Judith noticed that Wille had a large butcher knife in his hand (about a nine-inch blade).

Wille bent down and continued stabbing the hitchhiker. Then Wille used the knife to mutilate the hitchhiker's body, cutting off his jeans, stabbing the man in the crotch, and kicking the body with his foot.

260

Wood watched and listened to Judith's chilling description of the mutilation of the body of Billy Phillips, of the castration and the removal of Phillips's hand.

"Don't you see the hand that you wanted to touch your body?" Wille said.

Judith said she eventually was able to grab the knife and intended to kill Wille, but he overpowered her. He forced her to bend down on her knees next to the hitchhiker's body and to stab the body with the butcher knife. Judith said she was in fear for her life and complied, stabbing the body "many, many times," until she finally dropped the knife.

Wille then made her lie next to the hitchhiker's body and had sexual intercourse with her on the ground next to the dead man. After, Wille wiped himself with the hitchhiker's clothes and led Judith back to the little girl's body, which was now on the ground. Wille made her look at the body and made Judith touch the dead girl's leg. Then Wille raped the body once again.

Judith again explained about Wille leaving the pornographic books and magazines behind and described their departure from the area.

After Judith was taken back to her cell, the investigators went over her statement. Wood noticed the

261

effect the gruesome details had on everyone. A somber mood permeated the room. Policemen have always known how to crack a bad joke, how to use black humor as a release. But no one could find anything but complete depression in what they knew of the last moments of the life of Nichole Lopatta.

Wood's stomach burned with a strong acid taste. The coffee didn't help. As the men compared notes, someone likened Wille's and Phillips's attacks on the victim and Judith to the feeding frenzy of marauding sharks. The image remained with Wood. He knew that no matter what he did for the rest of his life, he would probably never face such evil again, such savage, inhuman brutality.

As an afterthought, Wood remembered thinking that if there was something more monstrous out there, he wanted no part of it. John Francis Wille was monster enough. *He was evil incarnate.*

Twenty-three

Monday, August 19, 1985.

In New Orleans, hair samples taken from the body of Nichole at her autopsy were turned over to the FBI Crime Lab by Carol Dixon of the Jefferson Parish Crime Lab.

At the Santa Rosa Jail, Judith Walters was interviewed again by FBI Special Agent Fred McFaul and Florida Highway Patrol Trooper Ed Redmon, as well as Larry Bryant. Again Judith was read her rights and waived her right to remain silent.

The questioning this day centered on the death of Frank Powe, a black male from Mobile, Alabama. Judith ran down, in detail, how John Francis Wille killed Powe. She and Wille picked Powe up hitchhiking on I-10 in Santa Rosa County. Judith said she'd been drinking heavily. They stopped for her to relieve herself in the woods. She was so drunk, she had a problem pulling her pants back up. Wille helped. On

263

their way back to the car, Powe said something about Judith's breast. Wille and Powe went back into the woods together.

When they didn't come out right away, Judith went in looking for them and found them both on their knees. Powe was engaging in anal sex with Wille, who saw Judith and angrily ordered her back to the car. Judith went halfway back to the car, turned and went back to Wille and Powe. At that time she saw Wille kill Powe with a hammer. Wille saw Judith, called her over to sit next to him while he continued striking Powe with the hammer.

After it was obvious Powe was dead, Wille turned the body over and performed anal sex with the body. Wille tried to get Judith involved in the sex act, trying to make her touch the body, trying to make her sit on the body. Wille tried sitting the body up and told Judith to have sex with it, but Judith resisted.

After, they put the body in the car. They drove a short distance, dragged the body out and left it in the middle of the Interstate. They backed the Chevy up and drove over the body at a high rate of speed and left. Apparently an eighteen-wheeler also ran over the victim later.

After the interview, the investigators compared notes. Armed with this information, Trooper Redmon would be able to close his case. They had a good autopsy on the victim and a good fatality report. The area where the body was found matched Judith's description. An impression in the victim's head matched that of a hammer blow. Of course, at the time of the initial investigation, after the victim had been struck by several vehicles, the police weren't looking for hammer blows.

Larry Bryant and McFaul were more interested in the modus operandi: Wille's trademark frenzied, marauding-shark sexual attacks on the living and the dead. It was a classic study of how a criminal's learned behavior evolved as the criminal became more attuned to his true nature. John Francis Wille displayed the characteristics of a sociopathic serial killer, a man with no conscience.

Tuesday, August 20, 1985.

At the Jefferson Parish Sheriff's Office East Bank Lockup, 3300 Metairie Road, Metairie, Judith Walters was shown a sock recovered from the vicinity of where Billy Phillips had been murdered. She identified the sock as one belonging to the hitchhiker she and John Francis Wille had picked up, the same hitchhiker who participated in the abduction and murder of Nichole Lopatta; the same hitchhiker subsequently murdered by Wille on June 2.

After the identification, Judith was driven from the lockup to retrace the route taken by Judith's

Chevy on June 2, after Nichole Lopatta had been abducted.

Judith successfully led the officers to the Phillips murder site and to where Nichole's body was found.

Wednesday, August 21, 1985.

While at the FBI office in New Orleans, Judith Walters told investigators she would like to make some changes in her statement that she provided to the FBI, concerning the murders of Nichole Lopatta and Billy Phillips. After she was read her rights again and waived them, Judith went over her story with SA McFaul and SA Terry Scott.

This time, Judith mentioned how Phillips told Wille that "he needed a woman of his own." After driving around the West Bank of New Orleans in the extreme heat of Sunday, June 2, Wille stopped the car. Phillips walked away and came back with a young girl. The girl, Nichole Lopatta, was holding Phillips's hand. She seemed willing and calm.

Judith added another new point. The little girl asked Judith if she herself had any children. This seemed particularly touching to the detectives. After pulling into an Exxon service station, the little girl told Judith that "Mr. John said we were fixin' to go where my mommy is."

Judith asked Phillips if this was correct and Phillips laughed, "Hell, we don't even know who her mother is."

Judith described the murder of Nichole as before, except she added that she saw Phillips carry Nichole's body after Phillips and Wille had attacked the girl. Wille then told Judith that Phillips wanted to have sex with Judith and Wille would never let that happen. After Wille killed Phillips with a knife, Wille told Judith, "Life is a bitch, isn't it?"

Monday, August 26, 1985.

Back at the Santa Rosa Jail, Judith Walters again spoke to investigators, waiving her right to remain silent. This time, she was interviewed by SA Terry Scott, JPSO Chief of Detectives Eugene Fields, and St. John The Baptist Sheriff Lloyd Johnson (the neighbor of John Francis Wille). Judith said that the information she provided in earlier statements was true and correct. She had a few things, however, to add.

She began by stating that on the evening of Saturday, June 1, 1985, she had taken her daughter, Sheila, to the Santa Rosa County Hospital in Milton, due to a bronchitis attack.

Judith then elaborated on the abduction of Nichole. After picking up Billy Phillips, she said, Wille and Phillips began talking about finding a little girl

267

to have sex with. They actually searched the West Bank for a girl Phillips had sex with once. Not finding this particular girl, they decided to find another one. It was Phillips who decided on Nichole.

Twenty-four

Tuesday, August 27, 1985.

At the Santa Rosa Jail, twenty-one-year-old John Francis Wille agreed to be interviewed by investigators. After being read his rights and waiving them, Wille spoke to FBI SA Terry Scott, JPSO Chief of Detectives Eugene Fields, and St. John The Baptist Sheriff Lloyd Johnson, along with one of his detectives, Sergeant Robert Hay. Wille said he wanted to talk about the abduction of Nichole Lopatta and the murder of Billy Phillips.

Cloistered in the small interview room, the investigators watched Wille, watched the smirky face, the dead, sharklike eyes, as Wille told his side of the story. Wille began by pointing out that the white Chevy involved in all of this belonged to Judith Walters. And, if the FBI found any blood and hair in the car, it probably belonged to Judith because Wille had beaten her often in the car. He described their numerous fights.

269

The Chevy was impounded by Santa Rosa authorities. Evidence was secured and handed over to the FBI. Then the car was transported, via U-haul truck, to the FBI Crime Lab in Quantico, Virginia, where a comprehensive search was conducted. This was expensive, but necessary, even if Judith claimed that Wille had used bleach to clean the interior of the car on several occasions.

Wille commented that he had lied earlier when he told investigators he murdered four people on separate occasions. "I like to bullshit," he claimed. He had not killed anyone at all.

SA Scott and Chief Fields advised Wille that Judith had provided details implicating Wille in the murders of Lopatta and Phillips. Wille asked if there was any physical evidence linking him to the cases.

Not yet, he was told, but the examination of the evidence was continuing. SA Scott did, however, point out that Wille and Judith had been picked out of a photographic lineup concerning the case.

Wille, in a cocky voice, said he knew nothing about the Lopatta and Phillips murders, except what he read in the papers and what investigators told him. Wille was aware that he had been placed at a Popeye's restaurant in Kenner on the night of the murders.

Wille went over the events of Saturday, June 1, confirming that Judith's fourteen-year-old daughter Sheila had become ill that Saturday night and had to be taken to the hospital. After dropping Sheila off at a neighbor's later, Wille and Judith drove to New Orleans. They had been drinking whiskey. They picked up a hitchhiker that Wille knew as Billy. During the course of their conversation, Billy said he wanted to "get a woman."

Eventually Billy got around to expressing his desire to have sex with a little girl around ten years old. He had done it before. They went to the West Bank of New Orleans and began searching for a little girl. Stopping the car in a residential area, Billy got out and walked off. He returned with a little girl five or six minutes later, a girl Wille said he now knew was Nichole Lopatta. The girl climbed in back with Billy and they drove off.

Later, when they stopped for Wille to go to the bathroom, Wille said that he saw Billy attack the girl. Billy took the little girl into the woods twice. On the second occasion, Billy murdered the girl. At that point, Wille said he figured Billy was going to kill him and Judith, too, so he "snapped" and became very angry and violent. He said Billy attacked him with a folding knife, and Wille had to kill Billy in self-defense.

Enraged because Billy had killed the little girl, a stone-faced John Francis Wille told investigators, he decided to cut off Billy's hand. While he was searching his car for a hacksaw, he saw Judith grab the knife and stab Billy many times. After, Wille indeed cut off Billy's hand. He later threw Billy into the water. Wille admitted the killings took place in the wooded area between Highway 51 and I-55.

He added that when he was released, he will find

Billy's grave and will use explosives to blow it up. "I do not regret killing Billy," Wille said.

After the initial statement was concluded, Wille agreed to give a taped statement, taken by Detective Sergeant Robert Hay of St. John Parish:

WILLE   We left here, Saturday night, about midnight, sometime during the night, early Sunday morning.

HAY   I take it when you say "Here" you mean Florida?

WILLE   Yea.

HAY   This particular county, Milton, Florida?

WILLE   Uh, huh.

HAY   You left Saturday night?

WILLE   Yea, and headed into Pensacola.

HAY   Who is "WE"?

WILLE   Me, Judy, and Sheila.

HAY   Alright, what night would this have been?

WILLE   The night that we took Sheila to the hospital.

HAY   Would that have been Saturday the first of June, 1985?

WILLE   Yea.

HAY   Okay. You all brought her to the hospital, what was the reason?

WILLE   Bronchial asthma, I think. I think that's what they said. She was having problems breathing.

HAY   Alright, go on.

WILLE   And they gave her some medicine. And they told us to take her home and put her in the bed, and Sheila's the type, she don't like that shit. We decided we were going to go riding.

HAY   And what was your destination?

WILLE   Oh, when we first left from Santa Rosa County our destination was Pensacola.

HAY   What was you driving?

WILLE   One 1976, Chevy, Impala, four door, white in color. . . .

HAY   Alright, go on.

WILLE   We got down there and we decided we were going into New Orleans, so we got on the interstate and headed towards New Orleans.

HAY   Interstate I-10?

WILLE   I-10. We seen Billy hitchhiking.

HAY   Billy Phillips?

WILLE   Yea.

HAY   Did you know this man?

WILLE   I had know him from before.

HAY   Alright.

WILLE   And he started talking about he was going to see some woman over across the river, so we figured we would take him over there. We got over on the Westbank and he starts telling me where to turn and shit, how to go. He told us where to get off. He was talking about, he knew this woman that was working and shit and she had some kids, he wanted to go see them. So I took him over there. He gets out the car and he goes to the door, he comes back with this little girl. I ain't asked him no questions about it and we start riding around and then we ended up in Laplace. And

273

that's when we were going down I-51. He tried . . .

HAY   Go on, John.

WILLE   He tried raping the little girl.

HAY   What little girl?

WILLE   The little girl that we picked up. He tried raping Sheila. He was saying all kinds of things to Judy. And I was having flashbacks and things, and Judy told me things that Sheila had said.

HAY   Like what?

WILLE   That her dad had tried to molest her when Judy was in the hospital in February.

SCOTT   Were you and Sheila with Billy when that little girl was picked up?

WILLE   When the girl was picked up, no, we stayed in the car.

HAY   Alright go on.

WILLE   Me and him started arguing and he had already fucked up the little girl too bad. He went at Judy and Sheila. I had a knife in my, stuffed in the back of my pants, me and him went a couple of rounds. He had a knife in his hand, he went for me and I got him before he got me. I ended up cutting his hand off.

HAY   John, was everything on this statement the truth to the best of your knowledge?

WILLE   That I can remember.

HAY   Prior to this statement you didn't mention anything about the hitchhiker, Billy Phillips, having a knife.

WILLE   No, I didn't, but he did.

HAY   He did. Alright, go on.

FIELDS   What kind of knife he have?

WILLE   A buck.

SCOTT   Describe it.

WILLE   It's one of them fold up ones.

SCOTT   How long?

WILLE   About six inches when you open it up. It fits in the palm of your hand.

FIELDS   What kind of knife did you have?

WILLE   A regular kitchen knife, that I always carried with me.

FIELDS   Describe it for us?

WILLE   About 12 inches long, wooden handle.

SCOTT   What color?

WILLE   Brown.

SCOTT   Where's Nicole when all of this started taking place?

WILLE   She had already been killed. He killed her.

SCOTT   How did he kill her?

WILLE   He raped her.

SCOTT   Raping don't kill you.

WILLE   He done it.

HAY   He what?

WILLE   Stabbed her because she kept yelling.

HAY   He did what?

WILLE   He killed her because she kept yelling.

SCOTT   How did he kill her?

WILLE   All I know, she was dead.

SCOTT   Where were you at the time?

275

WILLE   Trying to get my head straight.

HAY   Was he driving, were you driving the car when this was going on, were you stopped, or what?

WILLE   Yes, I was, I was driving.

HAY   So you're driving, where's Judy at?

WILLE   With me in the front seat.

HAY   Where's Sheila?

WILLE   In the back seat.

HAY   Where in the back seat? Right, left, center?

WILLE   I think she was behind me, I'm not sure.

JOHNSON   Where was Billy seated?

WILLE   I think he was in the middle, I'm not sure.

JOHNSON   Now, think good John. Think real, real good, to that point.

FIELDS   You say that Sheila was in the back seat with him while he was raping the little girl.

WILLE   He tried raping both of them.

FIELDS   Were you stopped at the time or were you still driving?

WILLE   Still driving when he started.

HAY   Did you let him do this now?

WILLE   I turned around and hit the son of a bitch once. He wouldn't stop. I just put the pedal to the metal and had it up. I got as far out of sight as I could.

HAY   Okay.

WILLE   I just stopped the car, he got out as soon as it stopped, dragged the little girl out.

HAY   And then what happened?

WILLE   I was trying to take care of Sheila at first and Sheila was getting hysterical, because she said she was raped when she was a little girl. It was hard to take care of all three of them at one time. I wished I could.

HAY   What happened then, John?

WILLE   I went after Billy with the intention to kill him.

SCOTT   What did you do?

WILLE   Knocked him on his ass.

HAY   How?

WILLE   First, hit him in the face and I kicks him and stabbed him.

SCOTT   Where did you stab him first?

WILLE   I tried cutting his nuts off because of what he had done.

SCOTT   That was your first stab? Where did you stick the blade in?

WILLE   I just swung it, didn't care where it landed.

HAY   Was he standing up or was he on the ground?

WILLE   He was on the ground.

FIELDS   Did you stab him just once?

WILLE   A bunch of times.

FIELDS   How many is a bunch? More than ten?

WILLE   Yea.

SCOTT   More than twenty or thirty?

WILLE   Yea, I just kept stabbing and stabbing and stabbing.

HAY   Who all stabbed him?

WILLE   Judy did.

SCOTT   Why did Judy stab him?

WILLE   Because he was fucking with Sheila.

277

HAY   Did you force Judy to stab him?

WILLE   No I didn't.

HAY   When was she doing this stabbing?

WILLE   While I was getting the hacksaw to cut that mother fucker's hand off.

SCOTT   Why did you want to cut his hand off?

WILLE   Just in case he didn't die, so the son of a bitch would never be able to touch any other girl.

HAY   Where was Sheila?

WILLE   In the car crying.

HAY   Did Sheila see this happening?

WILLE   I don't know.

SCOTT   Where was the car parked in relation to where you all was doing this fighting? How far away was the car?

WILLE   We were not too far away from it.

HAY   Was it in sight?

WILLE   I could see it.

SCOTT   Did Judy see you cut Billy's hand off?

WILLE   I don't know.

SCOTT   Did she help you cut his hand off?

WILLE   No.

HAY   Did you cut his hand off?

WILLE   Uh, huh, yea, I did.

SCOTT   What did you do with his hand?

WILLE   Disposed of it.

FIELDS   How did you dispose of it?

WILLE   A garbage can.

SCOTT   Where?

WILLE   Popeye's.

278

SCOTT   The whole hand or parts of the hand?

WILLE   The whole hand, I guess. I don't know, I don't remember, all I know is he's fucked up bad. He was dead.

SCOTT   Did you do anything to the other hand?

WILLE   I don't think so, I don't know, we may have.

SCOTT   Think good. Where did you put the body?

WILLE   In the car.

HAY   Where at in the car?

WILLE   In the trunk.

SCOTT   Are you sure it was in the trunk?

WILLE   I think, I remember putting one of them in the trunk. I don't know which one.

HAY   How did you get his body to the car?

WILLE   I carried it.

SCOTT   Did Judy help you carry the body?

WILLE   Just don't need any of her help, I'm muscular to do it myself.

SCOTT   I know you are, but. . . .

WILLE   Well, she didn't.

SCOTT   Think good now.

WILLE   If she said she had, that's a lie.

HAY   Did Sheila?

WILLE   No. Nobody did but me, myself and I.

HAY   What did you do after you put the bodies in the car?

WILLE   We got rid of Billy's body.

FIELDS   Where did you go to get rid of it?

WILLE   Over the bridge.

SCOTT   Who dumped Billy's body out over the side of the bridge?

WILLE   I did.

SCOTT   Did anybody help you?

WILLE   No.

JOHNSON   Are you sure that Judy didn't help you, John?

WILLE   No she didn't. If she said she did, that's another lie she's telling you.

JOHNSON   John, let me say something right here, you keep saying if she said this, she is lying. John, we are not trying to get Judy. You're not helping yourself by trying to protect anybody at this point. There are no plans for anything that I know of for Judy at this present time.

SCOTT   That is true. I know you love her and you care about her and you want to try and protect her, but she told us. . . .

WILLE   That's the only thing anybody can do to me is fuck over me and put her in prison, and I'll grant you there isn't a prison in this world going to hold me down if I ever find out she's going to prison.

HAY   John, we all know that this is hard on you, it's hard on Judy, okay, but you said you wanted to talk about it and you wanted to give a statement. You wanted to get it over with, is that correct?

WILLE   I do.

JOHNSON   Painting this statement with one lie ruins the whole statement, so when you are telling it, tell the truth.

WILLE Well, she did help me.

HAY She did help you?

WILLE Yea.

SCOTT How did she help you, John?

WILLE She helped me put the body into the car and put him over the side of the bridge.

FIELDS What did you do when you got back home in Florida?

WILLE Took Sheila and Judy home.

HAY Did you do anything with the car?

WILLE Yea, but not in their presence.

HAY Okay. What did you do and when did you do it?

WILLE I told Judy one day I was going to see a friend, took the car inside a set of woods and dismantled it. Tried cleaning it all up.

HAY What do you mean when you dismantled it?

WILLE I was pulling it apart, taking the rug out and all. Cleaning it up.

SCOTT Did it have a lot of blood and other things?

WILLE It did at the time.

HAY How did you clean the car?

WILLE Scrubbed it all out.

HAY Go on.

WILLE Put it all back together and went to see about Judy and Sheila. Just acted like nothing ever happened.

HAY Tell me what happened when you went back to your house.

WILLE   Sheila was asleep, I think, she wasn't no-where around that I could see.

HAY   Okay.

WILLE   Judy was in the livingroom, where we slept at. Nobody said anything for awhile. Least I tried not to, not at all, to nobody, I was too scared.

HAY   Okay, I can understand that. Go on.

WILLE   Tried to live like it never even happened.

HAY   Sheila didn't bring anything up?

WILLE   Not to my knowledge, not to me. If she did with Judy, I don't know. She never talked to me about any of it. Except we talked about her mama. Me and Sheila we had, we got this little joke, if anything ever happens to Judy, me and her are going to get married. Our own private little joke. And it seems to be taken the wrong way by Judy, quite a few times.

SCOTT   John.

WILLE   Yea.

SCOTT   Like I told you before, I talked to Judy. Did you at any time have any sexual contact with that little girl Nicole?

WILLE   No I didn't. Not at all.

HAY   How long did Phillips have intercourse with her?

WILLE   I don't know.

HAY   How do you know that he was having inter-course with her?

WILLE   She kept yelling.

HAY   What was she yelling?

WILLE   Pause.

282

HAY   John, what was she yelling?

WILLE   Please stop.

HAY   Please stop?

WILLE   Help me.

HAY   Help me? Did uh, were you driving at this time when this was going on? Yes or No?

WILLE   Yes I was.

HAY   Yes.

WILLE   Tried to get somewhere as quick as possible.

HAY   John, why didn't you stop the car and stop this?

WILLE   Afraid of what people around Laplace would think, because I'm well known.

HAY   What time was it, what was the hour? Was it day or night?

WILLE   Night time, I think.

HAY   Night time? Was it late at night or early?

WILLE   It could have been early.

HAY   Was it dark?

WILLE   Yea, pretty much.

HAY   Who would have seen this, John?

WILLE   It ain't no telling. Not as well known as I am, anybody could have seen me.

HAY   Can you look at me for a second? Alright, you are driving down the road, you are driving, Judy the front seat passenger, Judy's daughter Sheila's in the backseat, Phillips the hitchhiker is in the backseat, Nichole, the little girl, is in the backseat. You are driving down the road and this is going on and you did not

283

pull the car over to stop them?

WILLE   No, I was too afraid that somebody would see me.

HAY   Who would have seen you, John?

WILLE   Anybody could have seen me.

JOHNSON   John, you drove right on the side of my house.

WILLE   Yea, I did.

JOHNSON   You've been in my driveway a many of times. You know you could have pulled in there and we would have got the man and you would have.

WILLE   Too afraid what if my mom and them would think.

HAY   Let's rephrase the question John, did you at anytime this night, Sunday, the 2nd of June 1985 have any sexual intercourse whatsoever with Nichole Lopatta?

WILLE   No I didn't.

HAY   You did not.

WILLE   Not at all.

HAY   Did Billy Phillips?

WILLE   Yes, he did.

HAY   In your presence?

WILLE   Yea.

HAY   And you allowed Judy and Sheila to be subjected to this?

WILLE   I didn't want it to, I was trying to get somewhere's to handle it my own way.

HAY   Go on.

WILLE   The only place I knew where to go.

284

HAY   Which was?

WILLE   Out of the fucking town.

HAY   At what point did you stop the car, how long was Phillips having intercourse with this girl?

WILLE   A few minutes, at least five.

HAY   Her screaming and calling for help and asking to stop didn't affect you in any way, John?

WILLE   Yea, it did, I just didn't know what to do. There was all kinds of shit flashing through my head.

FIELDS   John, earlier when we were talking to you before we started this taped interview, you had made some remark and comment about Phillips dragging the little girl by the leg, was that true?

WILLE   No.

SCOTT   Are you sure, John?

WILLE   To my knowledge.

FIELDS   Did you see him strike her or hit her in any way?

WILLE   Yea, I did.

FIELDS   How did he hit her?

WILLE   He backhanded her.

FIELDS   Backhanded her.

WILLE   Yea.

FIELDS   How did he kill her? What caused her to die?

SCOTT   Did you see her die?

WILLE   Pause.

SCOTT   John, did you see her die?

WILLE   Pause.

SCOTT   John, you saw her die, didn't you?

WILLE   Yea, I did, but I didn't want her to.

SCOTT   John, how did she die?

WILLE   Billy kept trying to shut her up.

FIELDS   How was he trying to shut her up?

WILLE   Suffocate her. Cover her mouth.

HAY   With what?

WILLE   His hand.

HAY   Okay, then what, go on.

HAY   John, you said you wanted to give this statement right?

WILLE   Yea I did.

FIELDS   John, how did she die, you said you saw her die. How did she die?

WILLE   She's dead.

SCOTT   Yea, but how did she die. Describe it to us? What was Billy doing to her when you said he suffocated her?

WILLE   Trying to shut her up.

SCOTT   How was he trying to shut her up?

WILLE   Trying to keep Sheila off of him. Sheila was trying to fight him, trying to molest Sheila too. He was grabbing at her.

FIELDS   But how did the little girl die?

WILLE   I think Billy stabbed her, I don't know.

HAY   Were you parked or driving?

WILLE   When?

HAY   When the girl died.

SCOTT   You said you saw her die?

HAY   You just told us how you felt about Sheila right, you love Sheila?

286

WILLE Yes, I do.

HAY So a strange man or someone you knew vaguely is in the backseat of your car, trying to molest her — are you going to let this happen?

WILLE No I'm not.

HAY Would you speed up and try to get out of the way, so no one would see this or would you stop the car right there?

WILLE Stop.

HAY Go on.

SCOTT John, how did that little girl die?

WILLE I don't know. She was just dead.

HAY Who killed her?

WILLE Billy did.

HAY Let me ask you something, everything you said up to this point, is it pretty much it?

WILLE Best of my knowledge, yea.

HAY To the details and on the level?

WILLE That I can remember.

HAY You did know of this girl's abduction, Nichole Lopatta, you do know that she and Phillips were in the car that you were driving in Laplace. This is definite, no doubt. You are not making any of this up. Yes or no?

WILLE Yes.

FIELDS Describe the area where you picked the little girl up.

WILLE House, I guess.

FIELDS What?

WILLE Houses, you know a lot of houses

287

around.

HAY   Any business places around?

WILLE   Not that I can remember.

HAY   Did you all stop anywhere around that area before you picked her up?

WILLE   May have stopped at a Seven-Eleven and get some more beer.

HAY   Could you point out the area if you were to drive around, if you would see it again?

WILLE   I don't know! I don't know!

JOHNSON   Now, John, we are trying to get a true statement, don't get off on any tantrum. The more that you tell us the less people will have to be on that stand, on the witness stand. Like we talked about earlier.

WILLIE   I blocked a lot of it out, or tried to.

JOHNSON   We would all like to block. Judy is talking very freely to the officers, and the only other key to this puzzle is going to be Sheila. I know that you don't want to see that happen, because she would have to be on the stand. The more that you can tell right now and get the truth out in the open, protect, like you said awhile ago, if anything ever happened to you and Judy, you would want to marry Sheila, that's your own little, I know, that's a family joke, but you must have a lot of feelings for her, you don't want to see her badgered on the stand by some attorneys. So the only person that can keep this from happening is you. Now let's go back to the little girl dying in the car and take your time and do some thinking. Think about, you are

288

the only person that can help you at this time. Sheila, Judy and you were in the car, you are going to be a witness to a murder that Billy Phillips committed. That is your admission, but how did she die?

WILLE   I don't know. I really don't.

JOHNSON   You really don't know.

HAY   Were you present when she died?

WILLE   Yea.

FIELDS   Did you have any sexual contact with the little girl at all?

WILLE   No, I didn't.

FIELDS   If you did, would you tell us?

WILLE   Yea, I would, because to have any sex with anybody young at my age would be with Judy's daughter, that's one beautiful young lady.

HAY   Have you?

WILLE   No, I haven't.

HAY   Do you have any other questions to add in this statement?

FIELDS   No questions.

HAY   John?

WILLE   Yea I do.

HAY   Alright.

WILLE   If it come down to it and it was all happening again, I'd go about it different this time, totally different. With all this shit that's coming down here, I'd take my chances on getting my reputation ruined.

HAY   I don't understand.

WILLE   I'd stopped in the middle, where if somebody knew me, I'd take a chance that they'd talk bad

289

about me.

HAY   Is there anything else you'd like to add to this statement?

WILLE   Yea, if it come down to it again, I'd kill that son of a bitch again.

HAY   I understand that.

WILLE   Only because he deserved it. He deserved a hell of a lot more.

The major link missing from Judith's statement was finally put into place. Sheila had gone with them to New Orleans.

The statement had a chilling effect on the well seasoned investigators. Its effect was manifested in their quiet, stoic nature during the break after the first recorded statement.

Wille still wanted to talk, so the investigators continued questioning him about the Lopatta case, telling him how Judith had reported Wille's participation.

The investigators produced photographs of Nichole Lopatta and showed them to Wille. After looking at the pictures, Wille said that he had not told the entire truth about his role in the girl's abduction and murder. He said he was now ready to provide a complete truthful tape recorded statement.

The investigators broke out a fresh tape and began.

HAY   Alright. I understand that you would like to uh, add some details to your involvement in the case of Nichole Lopatta on this statement. Is this correct?

WILLE   Yes, Uh, Billy had fixed me a drink of Southern Comfort and Coke and it just didn't taste right. I didn't pay no really major attention to it, I just went ahead and drank it.

HAY   Uh, huh.

WILLE   I was pretty well drunk to begin with, I figured well what the hell, you know, it can't hurt.

FIELDS   When you said it didn't taste right, John —

WILLE   It didn't have the sweet taste.

HAY   How did it taste?

WILLE   A bitter taste, sour taste.

SCOTT   When did he give you this drink, when did he mix this drink for you?

WILLE   That was about, when we were still in New Orleans, we had just come back from the beach front.

FIELDS   This was before you picked up the little girl or after?

WILLE   He fixed me one before that too, I really didn't pay much attention to it.

SCOTT   Did it have that same kind of bitter taste?

WILLE   Yea, it seemed like every one that he fixed for me.

SCOTT   How many did he fix for you?

WILLE   About three or four.

SCOTT   That first one, was it before you picked up the little girl or after?

WILLE   Before.

SCOTT   Okay, go ahead.

291

WILLE   Uh, he had started talking about he had screwed several other young girls.

SCOTT   What did he mean by young?

WILLE   Around eleven, twelve, thirteen years old.

SCOTT   Okay, go ahead.

WILLE   Uh, certain things that he'd say, you know, would fade in and fade out.

SCOTT   This is while you are driving around?

WILLE   Yea, because I ran quite a few red lights, and that's unusual for me.

SCOTT   This is all on Sunday?

WILLE   Yea.

SCOTT   Okay.

WILLE   Now my driving to me, it kind of seemed like it was slow, now that I think about it. And I'm a heavy foot driver, you know?

SCOTT   Okay.

WILLE   You all ought to know from living in New Orleans, you know, you got to be good at the wheel if you want to stay alive out there.

HAY   Oh, yea.

WILLE   And uh, I don't know, it just seem like it wasn't me driving, I don't know. Just didn't seem like me, you know?

HAY   Uh, huh.

WILLE   Uh, he talked me in going to find this little girl, Nichole.

SCOTT   Did he mention her by name or was he. . . ?

WILLE   No, he didn't.

HAY How did he say it, John?

WILLE He said there was this young girl he wanted to go pick up and take her riding.

HAY Did he say where?

WILLE Not that I can remember.

HAY Okay, go on.

WILLE So we went over there.

SCOTT Over where?

WILLE He started giving directions.

SCOTT Are you on the Westbank now?

WILLE On the Westbank. We picked the little girl and started. . . .

SCOTT When, let's back up just a little bit, did Billy go pick up the little girl?

WILLE Uh, huh.

SCOTT Did you go with him?

WILLE I was there in the car.

SCOTT In the car. Who was with you in the car?

WILLE Judy.

SCOTT And?

WILLE Sheila.

SCOTT And Sheila is Judy's daughter?

WILLE Yes.

SCOTT Fourteen years old?

WILLE Yes.

SCOTT Okay. Did you actually see Billy walk up and actually get the girl and bring her back to the car?

WILLE I don't really know, I wasn't paying no attention to it.

SCOTT Okay. What did he do, I thought he . . .

293

WILLE   I remember grabbing, uh, I was opening a pack of cigarettes, uh, since, I smoke like a dragon when I start drinking.

HAY   Okay.

SCOTT   Then what happened?

WILLE   He come back to the car with the little girl and . . .

SCOTT   This little girl is Nichole Lopatta?

WILLE   Uh, huh.

HAY   Okay.

WILLE   And we just left and went riding.

SCOTT   Then what happens?

WILLE   Billy just talked about such and such, such and such.

SCOTT   Tell us exactly what Billy was saying.

WILLE   Asked me if I'd ever screwed anybody real young.

SCOTT   What did you say?

WILLE   I told him no.

SCOTT   Again, by real young, what did Billy mean?

WILLE   Around ten, eleven, twelve, thirteen, fourteen, I guess, I don't know.

SCOTT   What else did he say about that?

WILLE   He told me that I ought to try it. I told him it wasn't my game and it shouldn't be his.

SCOTT   Okay, then what happened?

WILLE   He kept rubbing, you know, saying you know man, come on man, don't be no chicken, come on do it, man.

SCOTT   He kept rubbing it in.

WILLE   He kept rubbing it in.

SCOTT   Okay.

WILLE   He seemed like a high school kid, you know talking all that shit.

SCOTT   Like a high school kid?

WILLE   Yea, like a young punk, you know like when you first get started in drugs, you know.

SCOTT   Then what happened?

WILLE   He ended up talking me into doing it.

SCOTT   He ended up talking you into it? Is that right? What was your answer?

WILLE   Yes.

HAY   What happened?

WILLE   All I remember. . . .

HAY   All you remember is what?

FIELDS   Were you in the car, out of the car, or where?

WILLE   Out of the car.

FIELDS   Where at out of the car, John?

WILLE   In the woods.

FIELDS   And who was there at the time?

WILLE   Me and Billy.

FIELDS   And who else?

WILLE   Sheila and Judy, they were in the car.

FIELDS   Where was the little girl that was with you?

WILLE   I don't know.

FIELDS   Nichole was with you and Billy?

WILLE   Pause.

FIELDS   Who took her clothes off?

WILLE   Billy did.

SCOTT   Did you and Billy have intercourse, sexual intercourse, screw little Nichole in your car in front of Judy?

WILLE   Not, that I can remember, no.

SCOTT   Could you have?

WILLE   Maybe, I don't know, you know, I was pretty well out of it. It wasn't me.

SCOTT   Tell me what happened in the sequence of events, who did what, when.

WILLE   Pause.

SCOTT   Will you do that for me, please?

WILLE   Billy screwed her first, then I did, then he did again.

SCOTT   This is all in her vagina?

WILLE   Yea, and then, you know, he kept beating on her, you know.

FIELDS   He kept beating on her.

WILLE   She wouldn't behave, she wouldn't be still at least.

SCOTT   Did you hit her?

WILLE   No, indeed, I don't believe in it.

SCOTT   Did you or Billy or both put your penis in her mouth?

WILLE   Billy did.

SCOTT   Did you?

WILLE   No.

SCOTT   Tell us what happened?

WILLE   She bit him, I'd expect any young girl

296

would do that.

SCOTT   What happened? What did Billy do when she bit him?

WILLE   Punched her.

SCOTT   Where did he punch her at?

WILLE   Punched her once in the head. She cried out.

HAY   Did he have his penis in little Nichole's mouth while you were having your penis in her vagina, was that going on at the same time?

WILLE   Yes.

SCOTT   Okay. Did you come inside of her, inside of that little girl?

WILLE   I don't know.

SCOTT   Did Billy?

WILLE   I don't know.

FIELDS   When he hit her and she started crying, what happened after that?

WILLE   I stopped, sat down on the side.

FIELDS   What did he do?

WILLE   He continued on doing what he wanted to.

SCOTT   What was that?

WILLE   Screwing her in her behind.

SCOTT   Was she still alive then?

WILLE   Yea, she screamed two or three times.

SCOTT   Did you see him actually insert his penis in her rectum?

WILLE   No, I didn't, I'm just, you know.

SCOTT   Okay. Did you insert your penis in her

rectum?

WILLE   No, I didn't.

HAY   What did she scream out, John?

WILLE   She called for her mama.

HAY   Calling her mama?

WILLE   Yea.

SCOTT   What happened then after he was having anal intercourse with her, what happened then?

WILLE   The more she'd yell the more he'd beat her.

HAY   And where were you?

WILLE   Sitting there freaking out.

HAY   Did Judy see this happen?

WILLE   I don't know. Really and truly, I don't know.

SCOTT   Did you pull Judy close? Did you pull Judy close to you and have her watch?

WILLE   No, I, I don't know.

SCOTT   Do you remember that?

WILLE   I don't remember doing that.

SCOTT   Did you ask Judy to perform oral sex on you, while this was happening, give you a blow job as they call it?

WILLE   Uh, Judy don't do that. Judy won't do it. She won't even do that in her own, her own bedroom.

HAY   Did she do this with Billy?

WILLE   Who Judy? She had better sense. That's not Judy.

HAY   John, where was Sheila at this time?

WILLE   I don't know. I know when we went back

to the car, there wasn't anything coming out of Nichole's mouth, she wasn't saying nothing or anything, not even moving.

FIELDS   Did she walk back to the car?

WILLE   She didn't go back to the car.

SCOTT   Was she dead?

WILLE   Yea.

SCOTT   How did she die, tell us exactly how she died.

WILLE   I'm not really too sure about that, really and truly, I'm not too sure about it.

SCOTT   Did you cause her death?

WILLE   No, I didn't.

SCOTT   Do you think you could have?

WILLE   I don't think, I probably, I don't know.

SCOTT   Think you could have and not remember it?

WILLE   Maybe.

SCOTT   Do you know how she died?

WILLE   No, I don't.

SCOTT   How do you think she died?

WILLE   He cut her, stabbed her, I don't know.

SCOTT   Do you remember what you told us before in your previous statement, how she died. What did you tell us then?

WILLE   Smothered to death.

SCOTT   And who smothered her to death?

WILLE   Billy.

SCOTT   Did that really happen? Did Billy really smother her to death?

299

WILLE   Pause.

SCOTT   John. How did she really die?

WILLE   I smothered her.

SCOTT   I'm sorry, I didn't hear you.

WILLE   I smothered her to get her out of her misery.

SCOTT   To put her out of her misery. You smothered her to put her out of her misery. She was in awful pain wasn't she, John? What's your answer?

WILLE   Yes.

SCOTT   Okay. Did you choke her or did you smother her?

WILLE   A little of both.

SCOTT   A little of both. Did you choke her first and then smother her, or did you smother and then choke her?

WILLE   Smothered her and then she passed out. Then I choked her.

SCOTT   And then you choked her after she passed out?

WILLE   Yes.

SCOTT   What were you doing when you choked her and she died?

WILLE   Pause.

SCOTT   Were you having vaginal intercourse with her?

WILLE   No.

SCOTT   No? Okay, what was Billy doing when you strangled her?

WILLE   Coming to fuck with Judy.

300

SCOTT   Trying to fuck with Judy?

WILLE   He was going to fuck with Judy.

SCOTT   He told you he was going to?

WILLE   Yea, he kept telling me that he was going to fuck Judy and Sheila. And I couldn't see it happening to somebody else.

SCOTT   Tell me about little Nichole after she was dead. Were you sure she was dead after you finished choking her?

WILLE   She just wasn't moving.

SCOTT   Did she ever move again. You have to answer.

WILLE   No.

SCOTT   Okay. Did she ever make any more sounds?

WILLE   No.

SCOTT   Did she have her eyes open or closed when she died?

WILLE   Open.

SCOTT   Open. Was her face badly beaten?

WILLE   Billy split her face a couple of times with his fist.

SCOTT   Okay. Did she have any other marks or bruises or cuts on her body?

WILLE   He was kicking her and shit.

SCOTT   Billy was kicking her?

WILLE   Yea.

SCOTT   Okay. Did you or Billy have intercourse with her after she was dead?

WILLE   I didn't.

301

SCOTT   You didn't. Did Billy?

WILLE   He disappeared for awhile, I don't know where he went.

SCOTT   Just disappeared?

WILLE   He just took off, like he went to get something or . . .

SCOTT   By himself?

WILLE   Yea.

FIELDS   Where were you at that time?

WILLE   Walking towards the car, back towards the car.

SCOTT   Did you really see him have any kind of sexual intercourse with Nichole's dead body?

WILLE   I don't think so, I don't know, he may have, I'm not sure.

FIELDS   That's not something that happens everyday, if it happened one time, you'd remember it.

SCOTT   Someone making love or having intercourse with a dead body, did Billy do that, did you see him do that? John, did you see Billy do that?

WILLE   Pause.

SCOTT   I can't hear you.

WILLE   Yes. It pissed me off.

SCOTT   You saw him have sexual intercourse with Nichole Lopatta's dead body. You said it pissed you off.

WILLE   I said, yea, I was sitting there just freaking out and I looked up and this motherfucker was back on her again.

SCOTT   Where is he, where is he inserting his penis?

WILLE   Up her rectum.

SCOTT   Up her rectum.

HAY   Up her vagina.

SCOTT   He was, he then had sexual intercourse in both her vagina and her rectum after she was dead?

WILLE   Yea.

SCOTT   More than one time?

WILLE   Pause.

SCOTT   More than one time?

WILLE   Maybe, I don't know.

SCOTT   John, did you?

WILLE   No, I didn't, not that I remember.

SCOTT   Do you think you might have?

WILLE   It's possible, I don't know.

SCOTT   Did Billy ask you to?

WILLE   Billy was saying try this, try that, try this.

SCOTT   Do you think maybe you did?

WILLE   As fucked up as I was, probably.

SCOTT   John, in reality what do you remember? Did you, did you?

WILLE   Pause.

SCOTT   I know this is hard, John. Did you have intercourse with that little girl's dead body?

WILLE   Pause.

SCOTT   I know it's tough.

WILLE   Yes, I did.

SCOTT   Want to say that louder please?

WILLE   Yes, I did.

SCOTT   Did you have intercourse in her anus after

303

she was dead?

WILLE   Pause.

SCOTT   John?

WILLE   Pause.

SCOTT   John, did you?

WILLE   Yes.

SCOTT   Did you have intercourse in her vagina after she was dead?

WILLE   Yes.

SCOTT   Okay. Did you have intercourse with that girl more than one time in each of those places, in the vagina and the anus?

WILLE   Probably.

SCOTT   Probably, okay. Did Judy see you do this?

WILLE   I don't know. Really and truly, I don't.

SCOTT   Did you have intercourse with Judy during this time?

WILLE   Pause.

SCOTT   John, did you have intercourse with Judy during this time?

WILLE   What me and Judy do, is between us and nobody else.

SCOTT   Okay.

WILLE   We got that thing that's in our bedroom or in the car, just us, nobody else.

SCOTT   Why don't you tell us about what happened that made you kill Billy Phillips?

WILLE   It just got me mad.

SCOTT   Why?

WILLE   He talked me into doing something that I

didn't want to do. And then he was going to fuck with my girlfriend and my daughter.

SCOTT   What happened?

WILLE   I flipped out.

SCOTT   Okay, then what happened?

WILLE   I started stabbing him and shit.

SCOTT   Where did you have the knife?

WILLE   It was in my possession, it was in my boot.

SCOTT   In your boot. Where did you stab him first, do you remember?

WILLE   All I remember is that I just went for him, and whatever I got was good enough for me.

SCOTT   Did you, can you tell us in detail, step by step what happened?

WILLE   I knocked him down on the ground and sat on him and just kept stabbing him, stabbing him, and stabbing him, stabbing him.

SCOTT   Then what happened?

WILLE   I tried to cut his prodicals off.

SCOTT   You tried to cut his what off?

WILLE   Prodicals off.

SCOTT   You mean his penis and balls?

WILLE   Yea.

SCOTT   Did you cut his penis and balls off?

WILLE   No, not all the way.

SCOTT   Alright. Then what happened?

WILLE   I got a hacksaw out of the tool box in the trunk. I cut his hand off.

SCOTT   Why did you cut his hand off?

WILLE   So if the son of a bitch wasn't dead, he wouldn't fuck with nobody else, bled to death.

SCOTT   What did you do with his hand?

WILLE   Kept it and disposed of it at Popeye's.

SCOTT   Where did you put it after you cut it off?

WILLE   Wrapped it up in some newspaper, I think.

SCOTT   And then where did you put it?

WILLE   In the car.

SCOTT   What did you do then, John?

WILLE   Pick him up to get rid of his body.

SCOTT   Now, before that happened, Judy was there wasn't she?

WILLE   Pause.

SCOTT   Judy saw this killing take place, didn't she?

WILLE   She may have, I don't know.

SCOTT   But, Judy was there, wasn't she?

WILLE   She was there with me, she was there in the car.

SCOTT   Did Judy do anything to Billy after you had stabbed him?

WILLE   She may have, I don't know.

SCOTT   John, did she do anything? Tell the truth.

WILLE   She stabbed him a few times.

SCOTT   How did she get the knife?

WILLE   I laid it on the ground.

SCOTT   Did you force her to stab him?

WILLE   No, I didn't.

SCOTT   Why did she stab him?

WILLE   I don't know.

SCOTT   Did this stabbing take place before or after you had cut off his hand?

WILLE   Before.

FIELDS   Did her daughter stab him?

HAY   The truth now, John.

WILLE   Not that I remember, no.

FIELDS   Did Sheila come up by the body?

WILLE   No, I don't know, that I can't tell you.

SCOTT   How many times did Judy stab Billy's body?

WILLE   That I can't tell you either.

SCOTT   Did she tell you why she did?

WILLE   No, she didn't.

SCOTT   Why do you think she did?

WILLE   Because the same thing happened to her when she was a kid. Because she told me that it happened to her, because of what had happened to her, and you know I couldn't . . .

SCOTT   Alright.

WILLE   She got her revenge.

SCOTT   You think she done it for revenge?

WILLE   Either that or her remembering when it happened to her.

SCOTT   John, did anything happen to Sheila with you or by you, by Billy, that night?

WILLE   No.

SCOTT   Are you sure? I can't hear your answer.

WILLE   Yes. I'd never touch my daughter.

SCOTT   Did Billy?

307

WILLE   I'd never let anybody else touch her.

The statement was sickening. Wille's new defense was that Billy talked him into it. If he thought this would pry any understanding from the officers, he was sorely mistaken. The description of the actual attack on the girl was more than monstrous. It fell on the detectives' collective ear like a visit to the infernal region.

Wille had also made it clear he was drunk. The investigators did not tell Wille that in Louisiana being drunk was not a mitigating circumstance; it did not lessen the degree of severity of a crime one iota.

While still in the interview office, Wille asked SA Scott, "If I told you that I think Billy put some kind of drug in my drink and that this drug could have made me do the things I did, do you think this information will help me?"

SA Scott told Wille the information would be put in his statement.

Wille also added, as a postscript, that he had indeed achieved sexual orgasms with the little girl both before her death and after.

Wille concluded with the fact that he was not sorry for killing Billy and that Billy deserved to die. Turning to SA Scott, Wille said, "I think I just put my ass in the electric chair."

As Wille's confessions were being taped, Judith

308

Walters was interviewed once again by Larry Bryant, Barry Wood, SA Vic Harvey, and SA Joe Hummel in a different interview room at the Santa Rosa Jail. After going through the constitutional rights formalities, Judith went over the activities of June 1 and June 2, 1985. This time, she included the missing part of her previous statements. This time she included her daughter, Sheila.

It was Sheila and Phillips who went into the apartment complex and came back with Nichole Lopatta. The little girl was holding on to *Sheila's* hand. Judith also admitted stabbing Phillips, but said Wille made her.

Twenty-five

Wednesday, August 28, 1985.

Back in New Orleans, the reinstated Lopatta Task Force received copies of Billy Phillips's record from the Office of Mental Health, Southeast Louisiana Hospital in Mandeville, Louisiana. Over two hundred pages long, this log chronicled Phillips's treatment at the state mental hospital dating as far back as 1980, and as recent as July 1984. Treated and released on more than one occasion, Phillips compiled quite an extensive mental record.

The recurrent diagnosis by several doctors described Billy Phillips as a paranoid schizophrenic, substance abuser, with a probable antisocial personality. This was listed again and again, as recent as June 1984.

Someone asked the obvious question aloud, "So what the fuck was he doing out on the street?"

* * *

Judith Walters provided a taped statement to SA Vic Harvey and SA Joe Hummel, Sheriff Lloyd Johnson, and Det. Sgt. Robert Hay at the Santa Rosa Jail. After going through the constitutional rights formalities one more time, Judith went over the activities of June 1 and June 2, 1985. This recorded statement took from 11:50 A.M. until 5:40 P.M. It covered five sixty-minute cassette tapes and was later transcribed on to 290 pages of typewritten text.

Throughout the statement Judith's voice remained strong and composed, ringing with its rural Mississippi twang.

Tuesday, September 3, 1985.

Barry Wood, along with fellow JPSO Detective Patricia Montecino, SA Vic Harvey, and St. John Detective Robert Hay, interviewed Judith's daughter, Sheila Walters in the presence of her grandmother and guardian, Patricia Hurst. The interview was taped. They didn't know at the time that this tape, more than any of the other taped statement, would play an integral role in subsequent court hearings.

Wood paid close attention to Sheila as she told her story. He didn't think he could be stunned again about this case, but he told Spade later that "Sheila blew my socks off."

311

In a monotone voice void of any emotion, Sheila told the matter-of-fact details of the gruesome rape and murder, as casually as if she was telling the story of a walk through the park.

She began with the night of June 1, when John Wille and her mother took her to the hospital for bronchitis:

Harvey: Did they give you medicine?
Walters: Uh-huh.
Harvey: Do you remember what they gave you?
Walters: Unh-unh.
Harvey: Okay, you got out of the hospital and what happened?
Walters: I went to sleep.
Harvey: Where did you go to sleep?
Walters: In the back of the car.
Harvey: Is this your mother's car you're talking about?
Walters: Yes sir.
Harvey: Alright, when did you first see Billy Phillips?
Walters: When I woke up in back of the car.
Harvey: Okay where, where were you, what city, what state?
Walters: New Orleans.
Harvey: Okay, was it light or dark outside?
Walters: Light.
Harvey: Do you have any idea what time of day it was?

Walters: Unh-unh.

Harvey: And you've been asleep until that time.

Walters: Un-huh.

Harvey: And you woke up and he was already in the back seat.

Walters: Un-huh.

Harvey: Was he introduced to you or, I mean, you just woke up and here he was?

Walters: He was there.

Harvey: Who was he talking to?

Walters: My mother and John.

Harvey: What were they talking about?

Walters: A little girl.

Harvey: What were they saying and, who's doing the talking?

Walters: Billy was talking about a little girl he knew and she lived in some apartment building in Terrytown.

Harvey: Did he say Terrytown?

Walters: Un-huh.

Harvey: Do you know where Terrytown is? Have you ever heard that expression before, I mean as a place?

Walters: No.

Harvey: Okay what was he saying about the little girl, do you recall?

Walters: No, all I know is he knew a girl.

Harvey: Alright, now when you got to the apartment complex you said you parked over by the playground.

313

Walters: Un-huh, yes.

Harvey: Okay then what happened.

Walters: Then me, John and Billy got out of the car. Billy had said something and John said something back and Billy said well there's the little girl that I was talking about and I'd gone up to her and I introduced myself. I said Hi my name is Sheila, and she said Hi and I had asked her if she knew Billy Phillips and she said no. I said well do you want to meet him because he said he knew you and she said yes and we was walking back to the car and she grabbed my hand and I was holding her hand when I walked to the car.

Harvey: Where were Billy Phillips and John Wille?

Walters: They had already gone back to the car, they turned around and went back to the car.

Harvey: Let me make sure I understand this, you all, the three of you got out of the car and walked into the apartment complex.

Walters: Un-huh.

Harvey: And Billy Phillips pointed the little girl out to you. What did he say when he pointed her out to you?

Walters: Well, there's the girl I know.

Harvey: And then when they turned around and walked away—

Walters: Un-huh.

Harvey: Did you go anywhere else in the complex?

314

Walters: I just walked up there and then we were walking back towards the car.

Harvey: Okay you got her, she's got a hold of your hand and you're walking back to the car and John and Billy Phillips are already at the car.

Walters: Un-huh.

Harvey: Where's your mother?

Walters: She was sitting in the car.

Harvey: Did she ever get out of the car?

Walters: No sir.

Harvey: Now then when Billy Phillips told you that's the little girl, what made you go get her?

Walters: I don't know, I just walked, started walking towards her and when I got there I introduced myself. I told her my name and I asked her if she knew Billy Phillips and she said no and we walked, we started walking towards the car and she was holding my hand and when we got to the car I introduced her to my mother first.

Harvey: What did you say?

Walters: I said mama, I said this is my mother and I said well what's your name and she said Nichole. I said well Nichole this is my mother, this is John and this is Billy Phillips.

Harvey: Did you say Billy Phillips or Billy?

Walters: Billy, I said Billy, and ah, John had asked if she wanted to ride to the store with us and she had asked us how long we were going to be gone and John said only a couple of minutes, so John told me to get into the car and he told her to get into

315

the car. John got into the backseat and Billy Phillips was driving, my mother was sitting in the passenger side.

Harvey: How's everybody sitting in the back seat, who's directly behind the driver?

Walters: John.

Harvey: Are you in the middle?

Walters: Un-huh.

Harvey: And the little girl is on your right, is that correct?

Walters: Un-huh.

Harvey: Okay and you all left the parking lot.

Walters: Un-huh and when we got to the store I asked her did she want anything to drink.

Harvey: What kind of store, do you remember?

Walters: No sir.

Harvey: Okay.

Walters: When we got to the store I asked her if she wanted anything to drink, she said yes and I got her a Coke.

Harvey: Did you get her a Coke or did someone else get her a Coke?

Walters: I'd gone into the store and put it upon the counter but John paid for it.

Harvey: And did anybody else get out of the car?

Walters: Billy Phillips, my mother and Nichole was sitting in the car.

Harvey: Okay, everybody got in the car, right?

Walters: Un-huh.

316

Harvey: Is the little girl talking or crying or laughing or what?

Walters: She is talking.

Harvey: Who is she talking to?

Walters: My mother.

Harvey: Okay.

Walters: And when I got into the car we left and Nichole, we'd been gone for a while I don't remember where we were going but Nichole said I want to go home now and John said why now? She said because my mother is going to be worried about me or something like that and John said well, you can stay out just a while longer, alright, just a while longer.

Harvey: You have no idea what time you all got the little girl?

Walters: Unh-unh.

Harvey: But it's still daylight?

Walters: Yeah.

Harvey: Okay, John and the little girl were talking, right?

Walters: Yeah.

Harvey: Okay.

Walters: And, um, she started crying and John told her to shut up, so me and her, we started playing a little hand game.

Harvey: Patty cake or something?

Walters: Something like that.

Harvey: Okay.

Walters: She said well, I want to go home now

317

and John said no and she started crying and John reached over me and hit her, I was trying, I was pushing John back.

Harvey: Where did he hit her, sweetheart?

Walters: On her arm I think, I think he had hit her on her arm and then he, she started screaming and John reached over and grabbed her arm and just squeezing it tighter and she is screaming louder.

Harvey: Are you crying?

Walters: I was screaming, trying to keep him off of her, pushing him back and Billy is still driving and my mother is trying to help me push John off of her.

Harvey: Is Billy seeing what he's doing?

Walters: No.

Harvey: He's just driving, okay.

Walters: Yeah and so John, we finally got John to leave her alone. She was crying, crying on my arm.

Harvey: Did she say anything to you?

Walters: No.

Harvey: Did she say anything to him?

Walters: Leave me alone.

Harvey: Okay.

Walters: Everytime she would say that John would hit her harder and squeeze her arm.

Harvey: Where is he hitting her when he hits her?

Walters: In her face, on her arms.

Harvey: Now when you say he's hitting her, how

318

hard is he hitting her?

Walters: Like he was hitting another man or something.

Harvey: I mean, he's really socking her, is that right?

Walters: Yes.

Harvey: Okay, alright go on, you're driving along, the little girl is crying, you're crying, Judy's trying —

Walters: We're trying to pull him off of her.

Harvey: Okay.

Walters: Well, she started, she started screaming and John told her to shut up and she just kept saying take me home, take me home, leave me alone.

Harvey: Is John doing anything else to her?

Walters: Yes.

Harvey: What else is he doing to her?

Walters: He, alright we had stopped.

Harvey: Did you all get out of the car then?

Walters: Un-huh.

Harvey: Tell us what happened then.

Walters: My mother and Nichole had gotten out and I had to go to the bathroom, so I went to use the bathroom.

Harvey: Where did you go to the bathroom?

Walters: In the woods.

Harvey: You got out, you got out to use the bathroom and your mom and Nichole got out.

Walters: Un-huh, and Nichole and my mother was talking and John got mad and I came out and

319

John and Nichole and my mother was already in the car.

Harvey: Okay, how did you know he was mad?

Walters: Because you could tell by the way he was acting.

Harvey: Alright you all got back in the car.

Walters: Un-huh.

Harvey: Was he still in the back seat with the little girl?

Walters: Un-huh.

Harvey: And the rest of you are up front?

Walters: Un-huh. And he kept on hitting her and I was up in the front seat trying to pull him away from her, make him stop hitting her but he keep on hitting her harder.

Harvey: What's she doing?

Walters: She's screaming and crying.

Harvey: Okay.

Walters: And I kept telling John to leave her alone, let's take her back home, just leave her alone, we kept trying to push him off of her.

Harvey: Who is we?

Walters: Me and my mother.

Harvey: Billy isn't helping at all?

Walters: No.

Harvey: Is he saying anything?

Walters: He just sits back, watching and smiling.

Harvey: I thought he was driving.

Walters: We had, this is when we stopped.

Harvey: Okay you stopped, what's going on in

320

the back seat?

Walters: John had almost had Nichole's clothes off of her.

Harvey: She's still fighting?

Walters: Un-huh.

Harvey: Is she crying or anything?

Walters: Yes.

Harvey: Okay you stopped, he's in the back seat trying to take her clothes off, there's you, your mother and Billy in the front seat, tell me what happens now.

Walters: John was trying, John was trying to have sex with her.

Harvey: What do you mean trying to have sex?

Walters: Well he, he was . . .

Harvey: He was trying to have intercourse with the little girl?

Walters: Yes, and by that time, we had stopped and Billy had gotten in the back seat and—

Harvey: Okay, describe to me what everybody is doing, where they are.

Walters: My mother is on the right side on the floor board.

Harvey: You're talking about the passenger side?

Walters: No, the driver's side.

Harvey: But she's in the back seat?

Walters: Yes. Nichole is laying down and she was still crying and screaming.

Harvey: What does she have on?

Walters: Just her shirt.

Harvey: Okay.

Walters: Billy was on his knees in front of her with his pants down.

Harvey: Okay, what's Billy doing?

Walters: Making her suck his penis.

Harvey: Okay, now then, your mother is on the floor?

Walters: Un-huh.

Harvey: That's a lot of people in the back seat of the car, isn't it?

Walters: Un-huh.

Harvey: Is Nichole facing up or down?

Walters: She kept trying to move.

Harvey: Is she saying anything or making sounds?

Walters: She is trying to scream.

Harvey: What is John doing?

Walters: He's having sex with the little girl.

Harvey: Has John had sex with her before this? This is the first thing you recall.

Walters: Un-huh.

Harvey: The little girl is still alive, right?

Walters: Yes sir.

Harvey: She's moving around.

Walters: Un-huh.

Harvey: Okay, what happened.

Walters: And then Billy had got up, walked around the car to the back where John was at.

Harvey: Now they're out of the car.

Walters: No, Billy is, he got out and walked

around to the other side.

Harvey: And you and your mommy are on the floor right?

Walters: Un-huh, trying to pull Nichole but —

Harvey: Let me ask you this, did you see your mom engage in any sexual activities with any of these people while on the floor?

Walters: No.

Harvey: Okay, what happened?

Walters: And, well, Billy Phillips was trying to have sexual intercourse with John, while John was having sexual intercourse with Nichole, that's when Nichole died.

Harvey: Is she still in the same position?

Walters: Un-huh.

Harvey: And he's choking her.

Walters: Un-huh.

Harvey: And where are you and your mother?

Walters: We're still on the floor, we're trying to pull Nichole —

Harvey: Trying to pull her away?

Walters: Down to the floor so I can get on her so they would leave her alone.

Harvey: How do you know, how do you know the choking killed her?

Walters: Because after John had finished, he raised up, he zipped his pants and he said "I told you I would do it" or "I did it" and I'm sitting here saying Nichole wake up, Nichole are you okay and she just wouldn't answer me.

323

Harvey: Okay, are you certain of those things that you're telling us?

Walters: Un-huh.

Harvey: Then you physically saw John choke her?

Walters: Yes sir.

Harvey: And the other sex acts, you were physically present?

Walters: Yes sir.

Harvey: Okay, after it's over, you said John is having sexual intercourse with the little girl while Billy was having it with him?

Walters: Un-huh.

Harvey: Describe that to me. How are they doing that, what are their positions?

Walters: I was still on the floor, my mother was still on the driver side in the floor, John had screwed Nichole up and Phillips, Billy Phillips got behind John.

Harvey: Phillips was in the car too.

Walters: Un-huh.

Harvey: Okay, so I can understand, are they on their knees or what?

Walters: Yes.

Harvey: So Billy is behind John on his knees, is that correct?

Walters: Un-huh.

Harvey: And John is having intercourse with the little girl. Have you ever seen two men have intercourse before?

324

Walters: No sir.

Harvey: How do you know that's what they were doing?

Walters: You could tell.

Harvey: You're sure, you're certain that's what they were doing?

Walters: Yes sir.

Harvey: Okay then after that, just so I understand, you heard Nichole and were able to talk to her until he strangled her?

Walters: Un-huh, yes sir.

Harvey: And then after that you were unable to talk to her any more.

Walters: That's right.

Harvey: After that time did she ever make any more sounds?

Walters: No.

Twenty-six

Wednesday, September 4, 1985.

John Francis Wille was indicted in the state of Florida for the murder of the black hitchhiker, Frank Powe.

Wednesday, September 11, 1985.

Barry Wood received a written report from the Jefferson Parish Crime Laboratory. According to forensic biologist Joseph Warren, a leading and respected forensic scientist, "Known head hairs taken from John Francis Wille showed morphological characteristics to a hair found on the victim's body at her autopsy."

Wood smiled to himself. They had their physical link now—a physical link between Wille and Nichole. Sometimes all it took was one strand of hair.

Thursday, September 12, 1985.

John Francis Wille, twenty-one, and Judith Walters, thirty-three, were indicted in St. John The Baptist Parish for the first degree murder and aggravated rape of Nichole Lopatta. Wille and Judith were also indicted for the second degree murder of Billy Phillips.

Friday, September 13, 1985.

Spade read the article in *The Times-Picayune:* "Two indicted in Nichole's killing." The large article detailed the intensive three-month investigation, describing how authorities from St. John Parish, Jefferson Parish, St. Charles Parish, the FBI, and Santa Rosa County, Florida, packed the St. John Parish Courthouse in the little West Bank town of Edgard, Louisiana, to hear the indictments read in open court. John Francis Wille and Judith Walters were still in Santa Rosa County, awaiting trial on the murder of Frank Powe.

"This is a notorious case," said St. John Parish District Attorney John Crum. Crum cited heinous acts, involving sex with a little girl, strangulation, brutality on the body of the little girl, and kidnapping. "Basically," Crum added, "it's pretty sick."

Spade wasn't surprised to see Jodee Lopatta's name resurface in the paper. The young mother said

327

she had finally learned the accurate details of her daughter's death only recently. "For three months I've been told that Nichole died from the first blow, that she died without any pain. It's very, very hard to find out what they really did to her. I can't fathom how anybody could do something like this. Nichole never had a chance.

"They told me all the times she lived, she cried out for her momma," Jodee told reporters. "I don't know why God allowed my baby to be hurt like that. Why did she have to suffer so much?"

The paper went on to elaborate on the crime again, this time telling the public how Judith's fourteen-year-old daughter Sheila had befriended Nichole and lured Nichole into the car.

Almost as an afterthought, the paper explained that the previous leading suspect in the case, although no longer a suspect in the kidnapping, and murder of Nichole, may still face charges that he molested several of Nichole's friends.

Bullshit, Spade thought. *The accusations of terrified little girls wouldn't stand up to serious scrutiny. No way.*

Later, on the phone with Barry Wood, Spade asked the question on everyone's mind, "So what about Sheila? She started the whole thing, didn't she?"

"The powers that be haven't made up their mind about Sheila yet," Wood said. She coaxed Nichole, knowing Phillips and Wille planned to have sex with her. She held Nichole's hand and sweet-talked her into leaving with them.

"Sheila showed no remorse when we took her statement. She was as cold as ice." Wood added, "Like mother, like daughter. If we aren't careful, she's going to grow up into another serial killer. She needs help. Somebody better see to it!"

Part Four

"It's never enough."

Twenty-seven

Monday, December 1, 1986.

After months of delays, the trial of John Francis Wille began at the St. John The Baptist Parish Courthouse in Edgard. In the new brick building, located a few hundred feet from the swirling brown waters of the big muddy Mississippi, the hulking drifter with the protruding Neanderthal brow was called to task for his actions nearly eighteen months earlier. Wille faced trial for the first degree murder and aggravated rape of Nichole Lopatta. He was also being tried on the second degree murder of Billy Phillips.

Wille had already pled guilty to the murder of the black hitchhiker Frank Powe in Florida, in order to avoid the death penalty in that state.

Jury selection began in Edgard at 10:00 A.M., in Louisiana's Fortieth Judicial District Court, Judge G. Walton Caire presiding, St. John DA John Crum expressed publicly that he expected the jury selection

333

in the "heavily publicized case" to take at least two weeks. Crum said he planned to seek the death penalty.

Crum described the case to the media as "a serious, complicated case, and not something that needs to be rushed into." Among the witnesses subpoenaed were dozens of law enforcement officers from St. John, Jefferson, St. Charles, the FBI, Santa Rosa, Florida, and the Louisiana State Police. Also subpoenaed were Judith Walters and her now fifteen-year-old daughter, Sheila Walters. Judith was still in custody, awaiting her trial in the murder of Nichole Lopatta.

Court appointed defense attorneys George Oubre and Robert Becnel had tried to postpone Wille's trial until 1987, but were rebuffed in their efforts by the Louisiana state supreme court. Oubre announced to the media that he only recently received information on other names of suspects in the slayings and alibi witnesses who might testify that Wille, Judith, and Sheila were in Florida on June 2, 1985.

Wille was finally moved back to St. John Parish to await trial, only he had to be housed in Orleans and Jefferson Parishes, because of prisoner reactions to his brutality to a child. Hard-core murderers and armed robbers wanted a piece of the now infamous Wille. Child killers were despised by all criminals.

Wille compounded his problem by gleefully telling the story of what he did to Nichole Lopatta. These retellings inflamed the parish criminals, who pleaded with their jailers to please, please transfer John Francis Wille to their cell block.

Tuesday, December 2, 1986.

Spade read *The Times-Picayune* article that morning involving the trial in Edgard: "Jury selection gets under way for Nichole Lopatta trial," tight security reported at the courthouse. After hours of "intense" questioning two St. John The Baptist men were selected for the jury.

Not bad, Spade thought, *for the first day of a trial of that magnitude.*

Like the two previous days' news reports, the paper ran a photo of John Francis Wille. In today's paper Wille wore a three-piece suit with a dress shirt and necktie. His dark wavy hair had been cut short around the sides, his square jaw neatly shaved. Spade noted how Wille's ears stuck out and his protruding eyebrows. No Robert Redford, Wille looked like a caveman in a modern day costume.

Defense attorneys tried their version of pulling rabbits out of hats, passing several motions in front of the judge in order to delay the trial, all of which were denied. Typically, defense counsels asked each prospective juror whether they had been victims of crimes and whether their sympathy for Nichole's

335

family would stand in their way of giving Wille a fair trial.

Among those dismissed from the jury pool by either side were a deputy sheriff, the judge's sister, a man who attended high school with Wille, several opponents of the death penalty, a woman whose sister was killed last month, and a woman who once voted guilty in a murder trial.

Spade remembered what a Jefferson Parish assistant district attorney had taught at the police academy. The object of the defense counsel was to confuse, to put up a smoke screen, to do anything to distract the jury (and the judge) from the facts of the case.

Spade figured Wille's attorneys had better bring plenty of smoke . . . *plenty.*

Spade picked up one interesting tidbit from the newspaper account. Wille's parents, Pat and John Wille, Sr., mingled with sheriff's deputies. Neighbors of Sheriff Johnson, their daughter was a radio operator for the Sheriff's Office. So, John Francis Wille's sister worked for the police.

John Wille, Sr., said he had no doubt that his son was innocent.

Friday, December 5, 1986.

The Times-Picayune, in its ongoing coverage of

336

the trial which had begun on Thursday, ran a large photo of Jodee Lopatta in its Friday edition. Jodee, wearing a turtleneck sweater, was photographed being comforted by another woman. Looking downward and to her right, the young mother was obviously in pain. The photograph gave the impression that the viewer was peeking in on a private moment, a moment of inner torment.

Jurors in a crowded courtroom in the small Louisiana river town of Edgard listened intently to the tape-recorded confession of a misanthropic serial killer. The coutroom's occupants were taken along a hair-raising excursion into a realm of brutality, violent sexual frenzy, and inhuman murder by the perpetrator himself, John Francis Wille.

Wille's confession was played in open court. The deep voice of the La Place man echoed through the chamber as he told how Nichole Lopatta was kidnapped, raped, and murdered.

Wille's mother burst into tears.

The faces of the jury showed little emotion.

SA Vic Harvey was selected to bear the brunt of the testimony duty for the task force. He was the case investigator for the FBI and would bring more presence to the courtroom than any of the other investigators, all of whom were glad to transfer the burden to Harvey's large shoulders.

Barry Wood quipped to Harvey in private, "After all, you FBI guys always get your man."

"That's the Royal Canadian Mounted Police."

"Oh."

Saturday, December 6, 1986.

In a creative move, *The Times-Picayune* ran two articles in Saturday's paper. One was entitled "Calm faces mask Wille family's pain"; the other, "Don't forget victim, support group says."

In one corner there was the Wille family, stoic in their support of the kinsman. Their lives shattered as John Francis Wille was accused of grisly killings, the Wille family had endured the natural depression that accompanies such developments. The younger Willes, ages eight, nine, and twelve, endured taunts and accusations by friends and schoolmates.

John Francis Wille's parents blamed Judith Walters for his being charged with murder. They reported to the paper that they believed John confessed to Nichole's murder to protect Judith.

The paper reported how the Wille family had maintained their friendship with Sheriff Johnson and other sheriff's personnel, that their daughter still worked for the Sheriff's Office. Wille himself "talks and laughs" with jailers "like old friends."

The Wille family was described as "sitting quietly,

338

waiting and praying."

"What's held us together is our belief in Christ and His will be done," Mr. Wille said.

Good, Spade thought to himself. *His will be done. John Francis Wille will be convicted and sentenced to death.* Spade wondered about the Wille family for a moment. He guessed it was like growing up to find your son Adolf decided to be *Fuhrer* one day, or your son David decided to become the Son of Sam, or your nice Republican son Ted, who'd decided he'd like to see more of the country, wound up leaving a bloody sorority house in Tallahassee, Florida, to capture national headlines . . . for years.

Spade felt little sympathy for the Wille family. From a large and close family himself, Spade could see how family closeness could tie people together during the worst of times. If the Willes said they loved their son no matter what he did, perhaps that could be understood. But what sympathy could there be in ignorance? They *believed* in their son's innocence. Maybe, just maybe, that was part of the reason John Francis Wille was as he was.

If there was one certainty in all of this, it was that the *only innocent* was a little girl named Nichole.

Barry Wood read the same article. He wondered what the Willes thought of their son's description of Nichole's murder.

339

The second article in the paper mentioned how Jodee Lopatta remained hidden from reporters. Without Jodee to illuminate, the paper centered on Elizabeth Harvey, forty-five, of Mandeville, Louisiana. Harvey, moving about the courthouse, said she was there to represent Nichole's mother until Jodee was ready to appear in court.

Harvey's own daughter, Faith Hathaway, eighteen, was kidnapped, raped, and murdered six years earlier. Harvey and her husband Vernon were members of a group called Parents of Murdered Children. They frequently attended trials with other victims' parents to lend support.

Barry Wood wondered again about a country where murder was that commonplace. He had testified in the trial, testified to the photographic lineup with Debra Davis. During his testimony, Wille just sat there with that same grin on his face. His attorney, Becnel, tried his best to shake Wood's testimony, claiming the lineup identification was coaxed. But Wood stood firm.

After the trial, he was informed by the prosecution that his and Debra Davis's testimonies were impeccable. The quiet and shy Debra was an excellent witness. She was unshakable.

* * *

340

Sunday, December 7, 1986.

On the forty-fifth anniversary of the Japanese attack on Pearl Harbor, the news media along the Gulf Coast echoed reports that John Francis Wille was found guilty late Saturday night in the sleepy town of Edgard, convicted of the first degree murder of Nichole Lopatta. Sunday, December 7, 1986 was also Nichole's tenth birthday.

The sentencing portion of Wille's trial was to begin immediately. Defense attorney Robert Becnel was quoted in *The Times-Picayune* as saying he wasn't surprised at the verdict. "It was what we all expected from day one when we saw the file. The tough part for the jury is going to be Monday."

During the trial, one of Wille's aunts described Wille as a puppy, ". . . easy to love and easy to touch." But she added that he was easy to kick and never got the love or attention he deserved.

Wille's mother claimed her son's life became troubled after his grandmother died of cancer several years ago. He became withdrawn. That was when his mother found out Wille was on drugs.

Maintaining her son's innocence throughout the trial, Wille's mother claimed he could not have killed Nichole. "He has two little sisters the same age, and he loves children."

Later, she changed. Mrs. Wille said her son should be punished for what he did, but not put to death.

341

"He should pay. I just can't see you putting him in the electric chair."

Talking later to Barry Wood, Spade learned that Sheila Walters had not taken the stand. Her attorney invoked the fifth amendment on the grounds that she might incriminate herself.

"So what's going to happen to her?" Spade asked.

"You got me."

Monday, December 8, 1986.

The Times-Picayune ran an article entitled "Lawyer saw another side of child killer." In the article, John Francis Wille's chief defense counsel, George Oubre, told about meeting Wille and how at first he didn't want to shake Wille's hand. "I thought he was an animal."

Spade, sitting alone in Morning Call Coffee Stand, said aloud, "Yeah, you're right. He *is* an animal!"

The paper reported that throughout the trial, Oubre was outward in his affection for Wille, sometimes wrapping his arm around Wille's shoulders or patting him on the back during the many tense, emotional moments.

"He's a nice kid," Oubre said. "He's had a tough life."

Spade answered the paper aloud again. "A tough

342

life? What about Nichole's life?"

"He can be as sweet, considerate, and compassionate as anyone I've ever known," Oubre was quoted as saying.

"Don't make me sick," Spade answered the paper.

Oubre went on. "The other day in the courtroom, when I started crying, he reached over and started comforting me. That's the John Wille I know, and that's the John Wille I don't want to die."

"All right," Spade said, "long as the state gets to fry the John Francis Wille who butchered Nichole!" He glanced around and saw that no one was paying particular attention to him as he sat along the center marble counter of the Coffee Stand.

Spade read the next article with increasing anger.

The article was entitled "Family, friends plead for Wille's life."

The story was laced with sobbing friends and relatives, a priest, a teacher, a sister, two aunts, and several family friends.

Wille's mother cried, "John is really a very fine young man. I love my son. I want to see him grow up and die a natural death instead of in the electric chair."

"Yeah," Spade answered, "what about Nichole? What about her growing up?"

Spade crumbled the newspaper into a large ball and threw it into a corner of the cafe. After finishing his coffee, he scooped the paper up and stuffed it in

343

a trash can on his way out.

Later that day, the same jury that convicted John Francis Wille sentenced him to the electric chair. Wille's father still maintained his son's innocence. He spouted off to the media that the state presented no physical evidence to show his son killed Nichole.

"They had nothing, nothing except his statement, which he gave to save someone he loved," said Mr. Wille, referring to Judith. He went on to say, "If in fact they could prove to me that he was there, I could accept the fact that he killed Nichole to put her out of her misery. I, my wife, my son, all agree that if we were there, and we would have seen whoever did it do it, we would have killed them on the spot, too."

Twenty-eight

Monday, January 19, 1987.

On Robert E. Lee's birthday, after months of court maneuvering, jury selection began in the Fortieth Judicial District Court of Louisiana in Edgard, for the first degree murder trial of Judith Walters. The presiding judge was Thomas J. Malik. Judith's attorneys had tried trick after trick, smoke screen after smoke screen, fast shuffle after fast shuffle in a vain attempt at delaying the inevitable.

In January 1986, Judith's attorney (former Assistant U.S. Attorney) Pat Fanning tried to get the trial moved, due to "prejudicial pretrial publicity." His motion was denied.

In July 1986, Fanning tried to get Judith's confessions suppressed. Again, his motion was denied.

In December 1986, after Wille was convicted, Fanning again tried to get Judith's trial moved due to excessive news coverage. Fanning also filed a motion to keep the state from producing evidence of Judith's criminal conviction record, as well as evidence that Judith had previously engaged in sex acts with a girl. The motions were denied.

Just before the trial was to begin in January, Fanning tried to get Judith declared mentally incompetent to understand right from wrong and to assist in her defense.

Two psychiatrists agreed Judith was capable of assisting in her own defense. They did, however, find a history of alcohol and drug abuse in Judith's past.

The presiding judge found Judith fit to stand trial. At the end of the hearing, he allowed her to talk to her husband. He did not allow Judith to see John Francis Wille, as she had requested.

Wille was no longer in St. John The Baptist Parish. In the custody of the Louisiana Department of Corrections, Wille was being prepared to be placed on Death Row. After his conviction in Edgard, Wille was indicted in Jefferson Parish for kidnapping, sexual battery, and cruelty against Nichole Lopatta.

Tuesday, January 20, 1987.

Judith Walter's gruesome confession concerning the last day of Nichole Lopatta's life was played in

346

open court for the jury. Judith wept while the recorded statement was played. At one point, she broke down, and the trial had to be recessed briefly.

The Times-Picayune's article the following day, entitled "Nichole slay suspect tells gruesome story," elaborated on all of the hideous details of the abduction, rape, and murder of Nichole, as well as the murder of Billy Phillips.

Wednesday, January 21, 1987.

Electrifying testimony marked the third day of the Judith Walters trial. A former cellmate of Judith's, Linda Pryor, twenty-five, of Virginia Beach, Virginia, was produced by the state as a "surprise witness." Pryor testified that Judith had told her that she had held Nichole Lopatta while John Francis Wille raped the little girl. This testimony was aimed at Judith's long maintained story that she was an innocent bystander.

Pat Fanning immediately objected. He said he had not been given copies of Pryor's statement. His objection was overruled by Judge Malik.

According to Pryor, Judith described to her the graphic details on how she participated in the rape and murder. "She laughed at times," Pryor said. "She acted like it was a joke."

Judith's defense centered on her being present, but not a participant. Pryor testified that Judith

347

spoke as "we" concerning her and Wille. "We did this and we did that. We used a hammer on her." Judith agreed to use Sheila to lure Nichole into the car, "Because they knew she wouldn't go with an adult she didn't know."

Judith told Pryor that she drove the car after Nichole was abducted, so Wille and Phillips could sexually attack Nichole in the backseat.

After the shocking testimony, Judge Malik issued an arrest warrant for Sheila Walters after she failed to show up in court. Prosecutors had called her to testify.

Detectives were immediately dispatched to Mississippi to pick up Sheila. Upon arriving at Sheila's grandmother's home, along with Mississippi law officers, the Louisiana lawmen found the house empty.

The angry lawmen were certain that someone had tipped Sheila off. This was confirmed by Laurel's Chief of Police. Occupants at the grandmother's nursing home claimed that the grandmother had received a call late the previous evening. The woman hurriedly packed a bag for her and Sheila and took off.

Thursday, January 22, 1987.

After a lengthy conference with prosecutors and defense counsel, Judge Malik ordered the jury to

348

disregard the testimony of Linda Pryor. The testimony was removed from the record. Pryor was declared "unreliable."

The able Pat Fanning had produced part of a letter Pryor wrote, claiming she had offered favorable testimony on Judith's behalf for $10,000. But all of Fanning's expertise, all of his bag of legal tricks, could not prevent the most damaging testimony from being presented.

Assistant DA Thomas Daley, outside the presence of the jury, said he had learned that Sheila Walters and her grandmother Patricia Hurst had left Laurel, Mississippi, Tuesday afternoon, "with instructions that their whereabouts were to remain unknown."

Daley wanted Sheila's testimony. He asked for a recess until she could be located. The judge denied the motion, but ruled that Daley could admit Sheila's tape-recorded statement of September 5 into evidence. This floored the lawmen out in the hall. Sequestered from hearing the testimony, word filtered out to them that Sheila's statement would be played.

Fanning went ballistic. He asked for a mistrial. "To put that statement into evidence without an opportunity to cross-examine that witness would be devastating," Fanning claimed.

Law officers in the corridor, when they heard Fanning had lost in his efforts to suppress Sheila's testimony, shook each others' hands. They felt certain that Fanning had just been nailed by his own trickery. Most of them believed it was Fanning who had tipped off Sheila and her grandmother to hightail it out of town.

Fanning told the judge he did not know the whereabouts of Sheila or her grandmother and did not instruct them to leave. Even if Sheila was present, he said, she would probably invoke the Fifth Amendment against self-incrimination.

But the judge countered that the FBI, St. John and Jefferson Parish authorities agreed not to prosecute Sheila if she were to testify. This was not entirely true. Barry Wood, who was at the recording of Sheila's statement, had not offered Sheila any immunity. He had simply gone to interview someone who was a potential witness. He had no idea, none of them had, about what Sheila would detail.

In a packed courtroom Sheila Walters's remorseless voice echoed as the tape of her statement was played for the jury.

After describing Nichole's rape and murder, the horrifying story continued.

Harvey: Then what happened?

Walters: Then me and my mom we had gotten out of the car and we had gone walking at this time and we were walking down the road. By this time it was pretty dark. We were walking and then Billy had come and called me and my mother's name and my mother turned around and said, what, and he

350

said you all come on back to the car. We're fixing to leave and so we went back to the car and Nichole's body wasn't there.

Harvey: Do you know where it was?

Walters: Not at that time I didn't.

Harvey: Okay.

Walters: But then we got into the car, I gotten in the front seat with my mother. My mother was upset and I was upset and so we drove off and I didn't know where Nichole's body was.

Harvey: Okay the four of you are in the car, right?

Walters: Un-huh.

Harvey: You, your mother, John Wille and Billy Phillips. Who's driving?

Walters: John.

Harvey: You and your mother are in the front seat?

Walters: Un-huh.

Harvey: Is Billy in the front seat with you?

Walters: No Billy's in the back.

Harvey: Where did you all go?

Walters: We had gone to this bar.

Harvey: Do you remember the name of the bar?

Walters: No, but I had to use the bathroom so I went in and I used the bathroom and I came out, my mommy was still in the car and Billy Phillips and John was standing on the other side of the car talking . . . me and Billy was walking off on the

351

pier and you know nobody was there and earlier when I first woke up, when we was on our way to where Nichole was, I told my mother that I thought Billy was cute and my mother told Billy and so me and Billy went walking and Billy asked me if I would have sexual intercourse with him and I told him no. He said why, I said because look what you did to that little girl. He goes, I know, I can't believe I did it either and, uh, well, he kept on trying to unbutton my pants and so finally we had sexual intercourse and then—

Harvey: Were you on top of the pier?

Walters: Yes.

Harvey: Nobody else was around?

Walters: No, and then we went back to the car and John and my mother was sitting on the car and we got into the car and went out on this road. I don't remember where it was but we went out on this road, it was dark, it was real dark.

Harvey: What was everybody talking about, did your mother ask Billy what he'd done to you?

Walters: No.

Harvey: Okay go ahead.

Walters: And we got to this certain spot, we all got out.

Harvey: Remember what the spot looked like?

Walters: No, a lot of trees around it, grass, I couldn't see much but John had gone to the back of the trunk and got a sleeping bag and I was still

in the front and Billy said come on let's go, so me
and my mother got out of the car, and we went to
where we parked beside the car and John laid the
sleeping bag out and again me and Billy had sexual
intercourse and my mother and John had sexual
intercourse.

Harvey: On the same sleeping bag.

Walters: Yes sir.

Harvey: Same time.

Walters: Yes sir.

Harvey: How many times?

Walters: Me and Billy twice and Billy made a
remark about he wanted to have sex with my
mother and John got mad and John said no, nobody else had sex with Judy except for me, she's
mine, and they got into a fight, an argument about
my mother. And John always carried a knife with
him, kind of a buck knife that you fold in and out
and John and Billy started fighting.

Harvey: John's got the knife.

Walters: Un-huh.

Harvey: Does Billy have a knife?

Walters: No.

Harvey: And you and Judy are right there.

Walters: Yes.

Harvey: How close are you and your mother?

Walters: Close.

Harvey: Okay.

Walters: John had stabbed Billy.

Harvey: How do you know John stabbed Billy?

Walters: Because I had seen the blood and could see the blood and, ah, he kept on stabbing him.

Harvey: Tell me, describe where everybody is right now.

Walters: Me and my mother is sitting together by the sleeping bag, him and John was up fighting.

Harvey: Are they standing up?

Walters: At first they were, until Billy fell on the ground when he was hurt, when John stabbed him.

Harvey: Do you know where he stabbed him?

Walters: No I don't.

Harvey: Billy fell down. Which way did Billy fall, on his side, face down, face up?

Walters: Face up, he was laying on his back and John sat on him and started stabbing him and then he looked at my mother and he said Judy and my mother got up and she went over to where John was, he handed my mother the knife and my mother started stabbing him.

Harvey: John was on his knees, is that right?

Walters: No, John was standing up then.

Harvey: What is your mother doing, did she get down back of him?

Walters: Un-huh.

Harvey: How is she holding the knife?

Walters: Like that.

354

Harvey: In one hand?

Walters: Un-huh.

Harvey: How many times do you think your mother stabbed him?

Walters: I don't know.

Harvey: What part of the body is she stabbing?

Walters: His chest.

Harvey: He's still face up.

Walters: Then John looked at me and my mother stopped and she looked at me and John said, Sheila. I said what? It's your turn. And I was mad because the first time I did not want to have sexual intercourse with Billy because I was scared that I would come up pregnant and I was mad at him because he made me have sexual intercourse with him, he made me sit there and watch what he did, what they did to Nichole and I said I don't want to do it and John said if you don't, I'm going to make you do it. So I went over there, got into it and started stabbing him.

Harvey: How many times did you stab him?

Walters: I don't know.

Harvey: Just a guess.

Walters: I just—

Harvey: I mean, more than five?

Walters: Yes.

Harvey: More than ten?

Walters: Probably.

Harvey: You were stabbing him with the same

knife?

Walters: Un-huh.

Harvey: Okay, was he alive?

Walters: No, he was dead when John got through with him.

Harvey: What else did John do with him?

Walters: After I left the knife in him, I ran over to my mommy and I was holding her because I was thinking why did I do that, I can't believe I did that, and we thought that Billy, well we thought that John had picked Billy up and dropped him but John had rolled him over and John was having sexual intercourse with Billy and Billy was dead.

Harvey: Describe the position.

Walters: Billy was on his back and John was on top of him, I mean Billy was on his stomach.

Harvey: John was laying on top of him?

Walters: John was on his knees behind him.

Harvey: Then what happened?

Walters: Then I ran to the car and then I saw mommy and John coming with the sleeping bag.

Harvey: How much time, how long after you ran to the car did you see your mother and John coming to the car?

Walters: About ten minutes.

Harvey: What was in the sleeping bag?

Walters: Billy Phillips's body.

Harvey: Okay, are they both carrying him?

Walters: Un-huh.

356

Harvey: What happened then, what did they do with the body?

Walters: They put it in the back seat.

Harvey: Alright.

Walters: And then we went to this other place, a little bit further down the road.

Harvey: Are you still on the dirt road?

Walters: Un-huh and John had gotten out and went around back and then to the trunk and he got something out the trunk. It was Nichole's body.

Harvey: You're sure it was the little girl's body?

Walters: Un-huh, yes, he brought her around to the front and he said come on now and I sat there for a few minutes and then mama got out and she walked with him. Then I went back there and she had none of her clothes on, John again had sexual intercourse with her.

Harvey: How was the little girl lying, face up?

Walters: She was laying face up and then when John got through with her he called my mother over there and he made my mother have sexual intercourse with the little girl too.

Harvey: Describe what your mother was doing.

Walters: He made her feel up her body, he made her touch her lower part of her body, he made her lick her lower part of her body and her chest.

Harvey: Okay, did he make you do anything?

Walters: No.

357

Harvey: Did you do anything with the little girl's body?

Walters: No.

Harvey: Okay, what happened next?

Walters: I was, we got um, I don't remember if they left the body there. I think they did, because that was the last time I saw her, Nichole.

Harvey: Did you stay there and watch or did you go back to the car?

Walters: And then I went back to the car.

Harvey: Did John tell you to—Sheila, did they make you do anything to the little girl?

Walters: No.

Harvey: Finish. You went back to the car right.

Walters: And then I seen John and Mommy coming back.

Harvey: And how long a time period was that?

Walters: About fifteen minutes later.

Harvey: Did they get in the car?

Walters: Un-huh and we went to, ah—

Harvey: Where is everybody sitting?

Walters: Well you couldn't get in the back seat because Billy Phillips's body was in the back, so all three of us sat in the front seat. I sat on the passenger side by the door, my mother was in the middle and John was driving. We went to Popeye's chicken.

Harvey: When you got to Popeye's, was the body still in the back seat?

Walters: Un-huh.

358

Harvey: Are you sure? It's okay if you're not sure.

Walters: I don't remember if it was or not, but John had gone inside Popeye's, he had come out with some bags and he had something in one bag and he handed it to my mother and my mother opened it and she started screaming and John just started out dying out laughing while my mother was crying and screaming.

Harvey: Did you see what was in the bag?

Walters: I got a glance of it but I didn't actually stare at it.

Harvey: Can you describe what you saw?

Walters: It was bloody, I could see that. It wasn't a good sight. I know it wasn't something that he bought at Popeye's.

Friday, January 23, 1987.

Judith Walters was convicted of first degree murder and rape by an Edgard jury of six men and women. The same jury, in the sentencing phase of the bifurcated trial, sentenced Judith to life imprisonment on both counts. The prosecutors said they were satisfied. "When you compare it to Wille's participation, I think it was a fair and just decision," said Assistant DA Robert Levenstein. Pat Fanning said he was disappointed, but not surprised by the

359

verdicts.

Walking from the courthouse, toward the levee where his car was parked, Barry Wood removed his sport coat and tucked it over his arm. He stopped and looked up at the bright south Louisiana winter sun. He shaded his eyes and thought, *It's not enough.*

He closed his eyes and let the sun's rays bathe his face. He knew it couldn't be enough, the trials, the convictions, the sentences. There was no satisfaction. Only justice, which cannot erase the pain.

He remembered her face, the delicate features, the slight smile, the honey-colored hair, the freckles on her nose, her dark and innocent eyes.

He let out a long sigh.

"It's not enough," he said aloud. He knew, in his heart, that in homicide . . . it's never ever enough.

Twenty-nine

Monday, January 26, 1987.

St. John The Baptist Parish authorities pressed their efforts on charging Sheila Walters. After all, they contended, she was the one who lured Nichole Lopatta to her death. Assistant DA Thomas Daley told the media that Sheila could be charged as a juvenile for her role in the kidnapping.

The Jefferson Parish DA, however, said it was unlikely his office would pursue charges against Sheila, even if the kidnapping took place in Jefferson Parish. DA John Mamoulides said that Sheila was in her grandmother's custody and was being cared for properly.

St. John warrants for the arrest of Sheila and her grandmother were still in effect. Mississippi authorities in JonesCounty informed *The Times-Picayune* that he warrants had not been served.

Monday, February 2, 1987.

Attorneys George Oubre and Robert Becnel filed a motion just before John Francis Wille was to be sentenced formally to death. Judge Caire postponed the formal sentencing and scheduled a hearing.

Oubre and Becnel claimed they had evidence from a Shreveport doctor who was a time-of-death expert. According to the doctor, who never examined either Nichole's body or the body of Billy Phillips, he was prepared to testify that the two died several days apart.

Oubre and Becnel further told the judge that they discovered that Wille suffered head injuries as a child. They wanted Wille to undergo neurological testing to determine his mental state at the time of the crimes.

Oubre and Becnel also claimed:

1. The prosecution did not present any physical evidence to show Wille is guilty.

2. The prosecution withheld evidence that could have shed light on Wille's whereabouts on June 2, 1985.

3. The prosecution presented evidence of Billy Phillips's murder during the Lopatta trial.

4. The defense was denied the opportunity to produce out-of-state witnesses who would have testified that Wille's confession was not voluntary, that

362

he was drugged when he made the statements to police.

When the motions were finally heard, after much bantering and legal maneuvering, all were dismissed.

Thursday, October 22, 1987.

The Jefferson Parish District Attorney's Office advised the news media that they would bring John Francis Wille and Judith Walters to trial on kidnapping, sexual battery, and cruelty to a juvenile charges involving victim Nichole Lopatta in November. Pat Fanning, Judith's attorney, succeeded in separating the trials.

Wille's new lawyer, Robert Pastor, filed a motion to suppress statements Wille gave police in Florida. During the hearing, Judith was called as a defense witness for Wille. On the advice of Pat Fanning, Judith invoked her right against self-incrimination and refused to testify.

Tuesday, April 12, 1988.

The Jefferson Parish District Attorney's Office without explanation announced to the news media that they would now dismiss all charges against John Francis Wille and Judith Walters. A week earlier, the U.S. Supreme Court refused to hear arguments on Wille's Edgard murder conviction, allowing the conviction and death sentence to stand.

Thirty

Tuesday, March 13, 1990.

The Louisiana Supreme Court ordered a hearing on John Francis Wille's complaint that no one told him that his court appointed attorney, George Oubre, was representing Wille as part of probation imposed after Oubre pleaded guilty in 1984 to making a false statement to a federal agency. Wille claimed he was denied effective legal help at his trial.

Wille's latest lawyer, Michael Fawer of New Orleans, said that the jurors should have been asked if they knew about Oubre's conviction.

Friday, September 14, 1990.

Five years after the murder of Nichole Lopatta, her convicted killer, John Francis Wille, entered the same St. John courtroom to seek a new attorney and a new trial. During the "Oubre" hearing, Wille took the witness stand. He said he would not have had George Oubre defending him, had he known of Oubre's conviction. "I felt very, very insecure and unprepared," Wille told Judge Caire. Wille, now sporting a full moustache and excess weight, appeared calm and collected, smiling for news photographers on his way in and out of the courtroom.

Oubre testified he did not bring up his conviction because he was ashamed of it, and did not want to prejudice the jurors by letting them know he was a convicted criminal. But he claimed he threw himself into Wille's defense, "consulting everyone," even spending his own money to attend a week-long seminar in Huntsville, Texas, on criminal defense work.

Monday, October 22, 1990.

Judge Caire ruled that John Francis Wille's attorney, George Oubre, was no hindrance to the defense. Wille was not denied effective legal help. Wille's arguments were denied. He heard the news back at his home on Louisiana's Death Row.

Thirty-one

Sunday, January 13, 1991.

The Times-Picayune ran an article entitled "Mutilated body found in St. John," in its Sunday edition. A woman's dismembered body, partly burned, was unearthed the previous day, after a hunter stumbled on the remains alongside Louisiana Highway 51 in St. John The Baptist Parish. The *Picayune* staff reporters, Bob Warren and Sheila Grissett, pointed out the area had long been an "unofficial graveyard for victims of violent crimes."

The latest victim, apparently mutilated elsewhere before she was buried in a hasty grave, was found partially wrapped in a dark plastic garbage bag, fastened with duct tape.

According to police, the woman's limbs were not "hacked" but were "cut" off. One of her legs was buried with the victim. Due to the unusually wet weather of that January, and the state of the body's decomposition, authorities speculated the body could have been buried for as long as three weeks. A nationwide missing-person alert was put out by St. John detectives.

Postscript

- Jodee Lopatta and her daughters, Jodee Bee and Samantha, no longer live in Louisiana.
- Jodee's mother, Eleanor Mallory, died of natural causes in June 1986, almost a year to the day after Nichole's death.
- Norman Gibbs no longer lives in Louisiana.
- Barry Wood is currently a special agent with U.S. Customs.
- Vic Harvey retired from the FBI and heads his own security consultant firm.
- Larry Bryant is currently a lieutenant with the Santa Rosa County Sheriff's Office in Milton, Florida.
- Robert Hay is currently chief of detectives of the St. John The Baptist Parish Sheriff's Office.
- Rene Stallworth is currently a detective sergeant with the Jefferson Parish Sheriff's Office.
- Lloyd Johnson is still sheriff of St. John The Baptist Parish.

369

- Harry Lee is still sheriff of Jefferson Parish.
- John Francis Wille is currently on Death Row at Louisiana's Angola State Penitentiary, awaiting execution. In 1991, "Old Sparky," Louisiana's electric chair, was retired. The mode of execution was changed to lethal injection.
- Judith Walters is currently serving a life sentence at Louisiana's Saint Gabriel State Penitentiary.
- Sheila Walters was never prosecuted. An adult now, her whereabouts are unknown.